Coated metal roofing and cladding

M. S. Oliver, J. M. Albon and N. K. Garner

British Board of Agrément

 Thomas Telford

Published by Thomas Telford Publications, Thomas Telford Services Ltd,
1 Heron Quay, London E14 4JD

First published 1997

Distributors for Thomas Telford books are
USA: American Society of Civil Engineers, Publications Sales Department,
345 East 47th Street, New York, NY 10017-2398
Japan: Maruzen Co. Ltd, Book Department, 3–10 Nihonbashi 2-chome,
Chuo-ku, Tokyo 103
Australia: DA Books and Journals, 648 Whitehorse Road, Mitcham 3132,
Victoria

A catalogue record for this book is available from the British Library

ISBN: 0 7277 2620 X

This book is published on behalf of the Department of the Environment,
Transport and the Regions (DETR) who funded its preparation. The views
and information presented in the book are those of the authors and not
necessarily those of the funding Department or the publishers. Not all
recommendations suggested are within the scope of the DETR remit.

Typeset in Great Britain by Tradespools Ltd, Frome
Printed and bound in Great Britain by Bookcraft (Bath) Limited

Contents

Executive Summary

1. The BBA was appointed by the Department of the Environment to conduct a detailed investigation into the performance, controls, standards and codes relating to organic coated metals used for cladding and roofing, and to make recommendations for the future direction of the Construction Sponsorship Directorate's support of the industry.

2. The materials most widely used for this purpose are coil-coated and roll-formed into trapezoidal profiles.

3. Some previous reports have led to allegations in the technical press that widespread problems exist with this type of product. This study did not bear these out.

4. Raw material suppliers, coil-coating companies and major roll-forming companies have quality management systems approved under ISO 9000, or are seeking this approval, and they cooperate with each other on development of new materials, difficulties in production, or failure in service.

5. Contractor members of trade associations are committed to follow codes of conduct, to use products complying with relevant standards, and to employ trained operatives, but few hold formal approval for their quality management systems.

6. A large number of contractors, however, are not members of trade associations and have no commitment to follow their standards.

7. The incidence of reported failure is low and indicates a failure to achieve the potential properties of current products rather than any fundamental deficiency in their performance.

8. Guarantees are available for materials, design and workmanship, both from the suppliers of steel products and through insurance-backed schemes operated through roll-formers' and contractors' trade associations.

9. Other coating processes and forming techniques are in use: the controls exercised in production are substantially the same as for coil-coated profiles, but the greater attention given to training installers of these specialist systems leads to satisfactory results being achieved more easily.

10. Some possible routes for sub-standard material to reach the market were identified. The customer is recommended to specify unambiguously the materials to be used to prevent product switching to an inferior material (using, for example, Agrément Certificates or the designation schemes defined in EN 1396 or 10169-1), to use the guarantees which exist, and to confirm that the material used is as specified.

11. The largely unqualified site workforce inevitably leads to some instances of poor installation which can have a direct effect on the finished job, even when good products are used. Careful selection of competent contractors is paramount.

12. The Latham Report identifies the need for site operative training and registration which is particularly lacking in roof sheeting and cladding fields.

13. There have been substantial developments in coatings, design and in alloy coatings for steel since 1976. These developments are largely covered in BS 5427, which has recently been revised and reissued as BS 5427: Part 1: 1996 and now includes a general description of the materials used and recommendations for the design of profiled sheet installations. It is regrettable that the standard gives little advice on fixings and rooflights (which are potential causes of failure), on the need for cooperation between different parties to the contract, and on the need for the owner or occupier of the building to establish a systematic programme of inspection and maintenance. However, in other respects the standard is considered valuable and its use should be encouraged.

14. Work on BS 5427: Part 2: Installation is proposed but has not started. Nonetheless, there is already a substantial body of authoritative guidance available on the installation of profiled sheets, and on the design and installation of other forms of coated metals.

15. European Standards are now available for the galvanised and alloy-coated steels and aluminium alloys used in coil-coating, and for general uses of coil-coated steel and aluminium.

16. Other European work is in progress on test methods for paints (including specific methods for powder coatings and coil coatings), external uses of coil-coated steel, metal roofings, sandwich panels, and powder-coated aluminium and steel. These draft standards encourage the suppliers of coated metal to establish the external performance of their products under standard conditions at defined exposure sites; the specifier is recommended to seek this information from the supplier and to ensure that it relates to the exact specification under consideration.

17. The technical benefits associated with the use of PVC are

considered significant, and the environmental case against PVC under current conditions of manufacture and use is considered unconvincing.

18. The technical benefits associated with the use of chromium in primers and pretreatments are high, the technical risks associated with its replacement by relatively unproven alternatives are considered high, and the risks to health, safety and the environment from the use of chromium in properly controlled automated plants are considered low.

19. The emission of volatile organic compounds (VOCs) from the powder coatings process or a coil-coating line (under current operating conditions where vapours are incinerated) is zero or low, and the use of these processes will assist the UK in meeting commitments on solvent emissions.

20. The international study showed that many companies in the field of coated metals are international in character, that technology transfer already takes place, and that materials and techniques in use in other countries are already available in the UK market. The international study also showed that defects in design or installation were not uncommon in other countries.

Acknowledgements

The BBA is grateful for the considerable assistance, cooperation and goodwill it has received in conducting this investigation from all the individuals and companies who supplied literature and responded to postal questionnaires, the building owners who gave permission to inspect their properties, and

Albright & Wilson UK Limited
Akzo Nobel Industrial Coatings
Becker Industrial Coatings Limited
British Coatings Federation
British Standards Institution (BSI)
British Steel plc
Building Research Association of New Zealand (BRANZ)
Building Research Establishment (BRE)
Butler Manufacturing Company
Cockerille Sambre
Coilcolor Limited
Colormat International
Courtaulds Nippon Paints Limited
Construction Quality Forum
Corrosion Maintenance Limited
Commonwealth Scientific and Industrial Research Organisation (CSIRO)
Construction Industry Board (CIB)
Construction Industry Training Board (CITB)
Das Leichtbau Kollegium
Decra Roof Systems (UK) Limited
Delvemade Limited
Department of the Environment Air Quality Division
Engineered Panels In Construction (EPIC)
Euramax Coated Products Limited
Euroclad Limited
European Profiles Limited
European Coil Coating Association (ECCA)
H H Robertson (UK) Limited
H H Robertson Germany
Hoogovens Aluminium UK Limited
Hunter Douglas NV
Hydro Coatings Limited
Kelsey Roofing Industries Limited
Material Science Corporation
Metaalunie
Metal Cladding and Roofing Manufacturers Association (MCRMA)

Morton International Inc
National Coil Coaters Association (NCCA)
National Federation of Roofing Contractors (NFRC)
Norwegian Building Research Institute (NBRI)
Pechiney Bâtiment
Peterson Aluminium Corporation
PPG Industries (UK) Limited
PPG Industries Inc
Pre Finish Metals Inc
Precoat Metals Inc
Precision Metal Forming Limited
Reynolds Aluminium SA
Sigma Coatings Limited
Stramit Industries Limited
TAC Metal Forming Limited
Talfab Building Products Limited
Thyssen Bausysteme GmbH
TNO Institute of Industrial Technology
University of Manchester Institute of Science and Technology (UMIST)
University of Sheffield
Valspar Corporation
Ward Cladding Systems

Programme

The programme of work was originally defined by the Department of the Environment (DOE). Its Tender Specification invited tenderers to propose modifications to the programme or to propose additional work; items 2.2 and 4.7 were proposed by the BBA, agreed by the DOE and were included in the programme. The programme agreed is described in Table 1.

As the work was conducted it was considered appropriate to expand the scope of Chapter 2 to include developments in design, and to adjust the structure of Chapter 4 to reflect the interrelated nature of work in CEN, ISO, BSI and by other organisations.

Table 1. Scope of investigation conducted by the BBA

1.	*Review of current practice*
1.1.	Review current practice of controls, approvals and defects feedback from manufacture to construction
1.2.	Identify any gaps in the approval systems
1.3.	Respond to any recommendations relevant to the cladding industry contained in the Latham Report
2.	*Trends in materials*
2.1.	Investigate trends in coating formulations and types considering the phasing out of solvent release materials under new legislation
2.2.*	Consider developments in metals and corrosion protection which may be relevant to coil coating
3.	*International comparison*
3.1.	Review relevant controls and approvals abroad (in Europe, North America and Australasia) as a comparison to UK practice
4.	*Current and proposed standards*
4.1.	Review current testing methods and their efficacies
4.2.	Correlate and rationalise test methods and make recommendations for standard test methods
4.3.	Consider British Standard updating requirements
4.4.	Review progress towards a CEN Standard
4.5.	Recommend an approach to addressing a programme towards supporting a CEN Standard taking into account the needs of the UK industry
4.6.	Taking into account the limits of the Construction Sponsorship Directorate's remit, formulate a programme strategy in terms of support for codes and standards and further research to ensure the quality of the product, including design, erection and maintenance
4.7.*	Take into account the expectations of owners and users for design life

*Indicates items proposed by the BBA which were not included in the original Tender Specification.

1. Review of current practice for coil-coated and roll-formed metals

This chapter considers coil-coated and roll-formed products, which comprise the majority of coated metals used for roofing and cladding. The control arrangements which exist within the coil-coating and roll-forming industries are reviewed; possibilities for cooperation between the different parties and arrangements for feedback on performance are assessed; and the role of trade associations and other organisations is explored. Gaps in approval systems are identified and shortcomings in the training of site operatives are reviewed in the light of the Latham Report.

Throughout the text references are made to certain proprietary products. Alternative materials with the same characteristics often exist. Any reference to a particular product is intended to serve as an example, and should not be construed as an 'approval' of the particular product cited.

1.1. Controls, approvals and defects feedback from manufacture to construction

1.1.1. Trade associations and other organisations

Companies in the coil-coating and metal cladding and roofing industries may be members of trade associations, may hold approvals for their quality management systems, and may hold approvals for their products through standards or technical approvals. Each of these activities imposes some form of control or discipline on the companies or their production. The particular role of each organisation, given in alphabetical order, is as follows.

BBA — British Board of Agrément
The BBA was established in 1966 and is the UK member of the UEAtc and EOTA. It issues Agrément Certificates for innovative materials not covered by Standards, and publishes its test and assessment procedures as MOATs (Methods of Assessment and Test). Its methods for coated metal for roofing and cladding are published in MOAT 34.[1]

Agrément Certificates are accepted by the Secretary of State as demonstrating compliance with the Building Regulations and have a similar status in Scotland and Northern Ireland. Agrément Certificates for coated metals[2] are summarised in Table 2 and are given in detail in Appendix 1.

Table 2. Summary of Agrément Certificates for coated metals

Nature of product	No. of certificates
Structural roofing systems	7
Pressed metal tiles	6
Coated aluminium coil	4*
Coated steel coil	4*
Powder coating	4
Other coatings (for industrial application to metal)	2
Aluminium – zinc alloy coating	2

*Each of these Certificates covers a range of coating types from the same supplier. Hence the four aluminium Certificates cover a total of twelve separate products and the four steel Certificates cover a total of 15 separate products.

BRE — Building Research Establishment

The BRE is the UK national organisation for building research, with a long-standing history of research into construction and fire. It contributes to Building Regulations (and many of its publications are called up in Approved Documents) and to British, European and International Standards. It gives advice on current materials and techniques in Information Papers, Digests and Good Building Guides, and covers its work in more detail in its Reports. The BRE conducted an earlier phase of the present investigation on coated metals.[3]

The BRE has established a building defects database in its Construction Quality Forum. (Relevant data from the Construction Quality Forum are considered in Section 1.1.3.)

BSI — British Standards Institution

The BSI is the national standards organisation for the UK and is the UK member of CEN and ISO. In the field of coated metals, BSI Standards produce product standards and codes of practice (which are considered in detail in Section 1.1 and Chapter 4 of this report).

The BSI offers Product Certification to product standards through the Kite-mark and BSI Quality Assurance gives approval for quality management systems under ISO 9000[†].[4]

CEN — European Committee for Standardisation
(Comité Européen de Normalisation)

The CEN is a federation of eighteen European national standards organisations and its rules oblige its members to publish EN Standards

[†]Throughout the report 'ISO 9000' is used to refer to the ISO 9000 series of standards, as a general reference both to ISO 9001 and 9002.

as national standards and to withdraw conflicting standards. (The BSI publishes ENs in the BS EN series of standards.)

The EC Construction Products Directive[5] identifies Harmonized Standards by CEN as one procedure to demonstrate compliance with its Essential Requirements. The European Commission has issued mandates to CEN to produce standards to address the Essential Requirements for a variety of product groups.

CIB — Construction Industry Board
The Construction Industry Board is charged with the implementation of the joint government/industry review of procurement and contractual arrangements in the UK construction industry. The mission of the CIB is to provide strategic leadership and guidance for the development and active promotion of the UK construction industry.

CITB — Construction Industry Training Board
The CITB is an industrial training board established as a non-departmental public body and founded in 1964 under the Industrial Training Act. Its prime purpose is to support employers in obtaining an adequate supply of people trained to appropriate standards to meet the needs of the construction industry. The CITB is supported by a training levy in the industry.

CONSTRADO — Constructional Steel Research and Development Organisation
See Steel Construction Institute (SCI).

CRC — Confederation of Roofing Contractors
The CRC was formed in 1985 and membership is open to all roofing companies (trade members) and roofing material manufacturers (associate members). The total membership is over 300, of which 46 are listed as suppliers and 59 state an involvement in industrial sheeting and cladding.

All members are advised to adopt the CRC Codes of Conduct, which cover:

(*a*) health and safety
(*b*) COSHH Regulations
(*c*) site procedure
(*d*) tenders and estimates
(*e*) working practice
(*f*) workmanship.

Other guidelines are laid down in the published Code of Practice covering vetting procedures required for membership, quotations, site supervision, completion of contract, complaints procedures and education and training.

Insurance-backed guarantees are available to all CRC members, but are not compulsory. The guarantee scheme comprises the following.

(a) The trade member issues a ten-year company guarantee on workmanship.
(b) A materials guarantee is issued by the manufacturer (if available).
(c) An insurance-backed insolvency guarantee to cover the trade member is available from the insurance brokers of the CRC.

CWCT — Centre for Window and Cladding Technology

The CWCT is sponsored by the window and cladding industry, conducts research, gives training and education, publishes guidelines on the design, fabrication and installation of cladding, curtain walling and windows,[6] and is located at the University of Bath in the UK.

ECCA — European Coil Coating Association

The ECCA was established in 1967 and has 198 member companies. It represents different interests in coil coating within and outside Europe; its membership is summarised in Table 3.

The aims of the ECCA are to develop and promote a sound technical basis for the production and use of coated coil. Its technical activities are handled by building, environmental, quality and exposure task groups. Through these groups the ECCA has developed its own test methods for use in production and development,[7] has promoted the use of four natural exposure test stations in Europe,[8] has published recommendations on the maintenance of installations of coated metals[9] and sits on European Standards committees for coated steel and aluminium in building applications.

Table 3. Membership of the European Coil Coating Association (1996)

	UK* members	Europe (outside UK)	Outside Europe
Coil coaters	7	45	18
Paint suppliers	9	39	11
Pretreatment chemicals	3	13	—
Manufacturers of coil-coating systems	2	11	1
Film suppliers	1	7	—
Steel suppliers	—	7	2
Other categories†	1	19	2

*Some 'European' entries trade in the UK but do not have separate ECCA membership.
†'Other categories' includes national associations and manufacturers of polymers, pigments, test equipment, temporary protective film and adhesives.

ECCS — European Convention for Constructional Steelwork
The ECCS was formed in 1955 and comprises 19 structural steelwork trade associations. Its aim is to promote the efficient use of structural steelwork and it achieves this through its own published recommendations/design manuals[10] and through its work on European committees. The British Constructional Steelwork Association (BCSA) is the UK member of the ECCS, and ECCS publications are available from the BCSA or the Steel Construction Institute.

ECISS — European Committee for Iron and Steel Standardisation
Traditionally, European standardisation for coal and steel has been handled by the European Coal and Steel Community as an activity of the European Commission, which issued its standards as Euronorms,[11] independently of CEN. The ECISS has adopted this activity and uses CEN's Unique Acceptance Procedure to submit its standards to CEN's voting procedures, and standards for steel products are now issued as ENs (with numbers above EN 10000).

EOTA — European Organisation for Technical Approvals
The EC Construction Products Directive[5] identified two procedures for a product to demonstrate its compliance with the Essential Requirements. Where a Harmonized Standard does not exist or is inappropriate, a product can demonstrate its compliance with the Essential Requirements by a direct evaluation of its performance in a European Technical Approval. EOTA comprises the national authorities in the EC which issue European Technical Approvals.

EPIC — Engineered Panels in Construction
EPIC was set up in 1991 and includes the four members of MCRMA (see below) who produce composite panels (with metal facings and an insulating polyurethane or polyisocyanurate foam core). Its role is to give advice on the use of these materials.

ISO — International Organisation for Standardisation
ISO is a world-wide federation of national standards organisations. Unlike CEN's procedures, its members are not obliged to publish ISOs as national standards. Until CEN's status changed with the emphasis on Harmonized ENs given by the EC Construction Products Directive,[5] CEN would not handle work which ISO was already conducting. With CEN's present position, CEN and ISO have developed procedures to avoid conflict and duplication of work, which are described in the 'Vienna Agreement'.[12]

The BSI publish ISOs in the BS ISO series. Where the same text has been accepted both as an ISO and EN, BSI publish this in the BS EN ISO series.

MCRMA — *Metal Cladding and Roofing Manufacturers Association*

The MCRMA was established in 1989 and currently has 14 full-member companies — all UK producers of roll-formed metal roofing and cladding, secret-fix systems or composite panels. (Manufacturers of fixings, rooflights, etc. are able to join as associate members.) The Association's aim is to improve and disseminate technical knowledge within the industry. It has produced a series of technical papers/design guides[13], is a member of the European Profiles and Panels Federation and sits on European Standards Committees for coated metal cladding and roofing.

Members of MCRMA are committed to a Membership Charter which commits them to

(a) operate a quality management system approved under ISO 9000 (or to seek it and achieve it within two years)

(b) use materials from companies with a quality management system approved to ISO 9000 (and provide Certificates of Origin on the raw materials* if asked to do so)

(c) observe the manufacturing tolerances for profiles defined in MCRMA '*Manufacturing Tolerances for Profiled Metal Roof and Wall Cladding*'[13]

(d) use internationally recognised calculations or test data in preparing load–span tables

(e) employ qualified engineers to provide design guidance to specifiers and contractors and to register these employees with the MCRMA

(f) offer advice on appropriate installers*

(g) offer guidance on an appropriate third party who can be consulted in the event of a dispute

(h) brand their products so that they can be identified.

MCRMA members are able to offer latent defects insurance on a cladding or roofing installation. This is offered subject to a technical audit by TBV Surveying which

(a) establishes whether the design is conventional (i.e. without features with abnormal risks of failure)

---

*The Membership Charter was examined and accepted by the Office of Fair Trading (OFT). The provision of Certificates of Origin (b) is a requirement of the OFT, but the OFT does not accept the practice of MCRMA members giving installers 'approved installer' status, so the MCRMA considers their members' role (f) is restricted to giving advice on appropriate installers.

(b) confirms that supervision, materials and workmanship meet the proposed standards

(c) conducts a waterproofing check on the completed installation.

The insurance offered is for ten years and covers

(a) structural defects and fixing to the building
(b) water ingress after the first twelve months
(c) latent defects due to design, workmanship or materials
(d) change of ownership, i.e. can be assigned to future owners or tenants
(e) remedial work, enabling it to take place before liability is assigned.

NFRC — National Federation of Roofing Contractors

Full membership of the NFRC is open to roofing contractors and the NFRC has over 600 members in all roofing trades. Two hundred and six companies are listed for industrial roofing and cladding (166 operating from one location, 13 companies with more than one branch office, 35 branch offices in total). Associate membership is open to suppliers of roofing materials, and 16 suppliers of metal roofing and cladding, three suppliers of composite panels and five suppliers of pressed metal tiles are listed as associate members (seven of these companies are also members of the MCRMA).

The NFRC has a technical committee made up of contractors and suppliers which deals exclusively with sheeting and cladding matters. The NFRC cooperates on training with the Construction Industry Training Board, is represented on BSI and CEN Committees by trade, associate members or officers, and has produced its own *Guide to Good Practice for Profiled Metal Sheet Roofing and Cladding*,[14] which is under revision and will be reissued in 1998.

Members of the NFRC are committed to a Code of Conduct which commits them to

(a) transparent terms of Contract
(b) clear specifications and quotations for work
(c) conduct work with trained operatives, together with properly supervised labourers and apprentices
(d) use products complying with relevant British or European Standards
(e) follow relevant technical approvals, codes of practice and health and safety regulations
(f) inspect new work within one month of completion and rectify if necessary
(g) offer conciliation or arbitration in the event of a dispute and abide by the findings of a separate NFRC member appointed to investigate the Contract in dispute.

By following the Code of Conduct, NFRC members are able to offer the NFRC Co-Partnership Insurance Guarantee, which covers ten years and includes

(*a*)   a guarantee from the contactor which covers the work
(*b*)   a guarantee from the supplier (i.e. the NFRC Associate Member) which covers the materials
(*c*)   an underwritten insolvency guarantee, backed by insurance, against the contractor or supplier going out of business.

SCI — Steel Construction Institute

The Steel Construction Institute was founded in 1986 and its aims are to develop and promote the use of steel in construction, through research and publications. (Before 1986 the same role was undertaken by Constrado, the Constructional Steel Research and Development Organisation.)

UEAtc — European Union of Agrément

The UEAtc comprises Agrément authorities in Western Europe who issue approvals for innovative materials on the basis of their 'fitness for purpose'. The UEAtc previously issued Technical Guides, agreed test methods and procedures for assessing materials not covered by standards. It now issues Technical Reports, which give the general principles its members should use in their assessments of particular new materials and techniques and has prepared a *Technical Report for the Assessment of Installations using Sandwich Panels with a CFC-free PUR foam core*,[15] with the cooperation of the European Profiles and Panels Federation.

Other Quality Assurance Organisations

Other organisations (besides BSI QA) which are accredited to give approval for quality management systems under the ISO 9000 series are Bureau Veritas QI, Lloyds Register Quality Assurance, the Steel Construction QA scheme, UK CARES, Yarsley Quality Assurance and national bodies in other countries.

1.1.2. Investigations of supply chain from manufacture to construction

Four parties can be identified in the supply chain for coil-coated and roll-formed metals which is illustrated in Figure 1.

The supply chain thus comprises

(*a*)   suppliers of metal coil, coatings and pretreatment chemicals
(*b*)   coil coaters who combine these materials into the coated coil
(*c*)   roll-forming companies who convert the coated coil into profiles and the flashings and fittings which are used with them

(d)   contractors who install the profiled sheet and the necessary flashings and fittings.

The BBA conducted a postal survey with different surveys sent to the different parties involved in the separate stages of the process. The results of the surveys are summarised in Appendix 2. Certain questions addressed the controls, approvals and defects feedback procedures of the different parties, and the questionnaires were structured to show whether and how each party would cooperate with the customer/supplier in the event of difficulties in production or failure in service. The questions included some emphasis on formal quality management systems under the ISO 9000 series. The particular standards which have a bearing on this work are ISO 9001 and ISO 9002.[4] The relevant clauses (which are the same in both standards) are listed in Table 4.

The BBA also made visits to a selection of companies involved in the various processes to explore their role in greater depth.

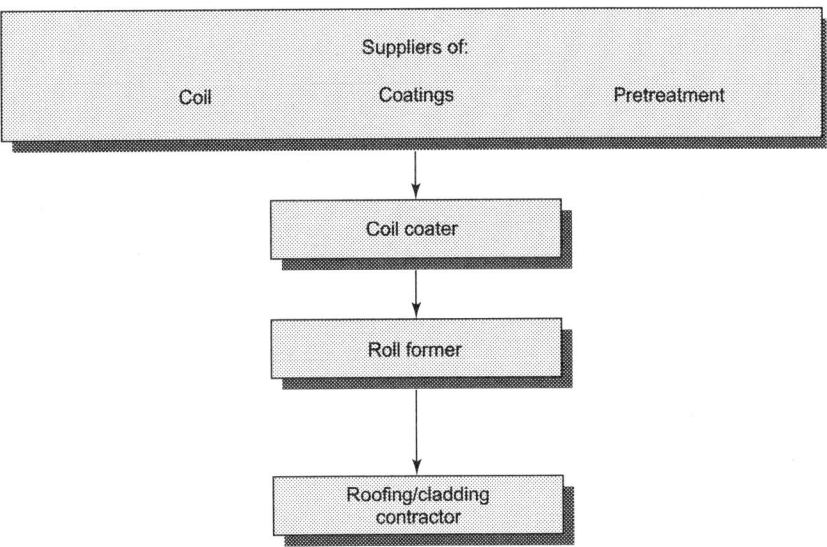

Figure 1. Supply chain from manufacture to construction

Table 4. Relevant requirements of ISO 9001 and ISO 9002

Requirement	Clause (ISO 9001) (ISO 9002)
Product to have a distinct identity, to be traceable through production, delivery and installation	4.8
Procedures for investigating complaints and taking appropriate action	4.14
Records to be maintained	4.16

Suppliers of metal coil

Questionnaires were sent to two suppliers of steel coil and to one supplier of aluminium coil, but no replies were received. Separate questionnaires were sent to twelve coil-coating companies and seven replies were received. These included a question which asked whether their procedures were covered by ISO 9000. Visits were made to two coil-coating companies and the details on manufacture given in seven Agrément Certificates held by coil-coating companies were examined. The findings were as follows.

Controls and complaint procedures are already well established in the metal supply industry and pre-date the issue of formal quality assurance standards such as BS 5750. Manufacturers of metal coil have sought and achieved approval for their quality management system under ISO 9000 as a matter of routine. Furthermore, there is some vertical integration within the industry and some coil-coating and roll-forming companies are subsidiaries of steel or aluminium producers.

The survey of coil-coating companies showed that six companies (of the seven who replied) had quality management systems approved under ISO 9000 (which includes a requirement for the materials used to be 'traceable') and that the remaining company was seeking approval. Visits to coil-coating companies showed that these ISO 9000 procedures included some discrimination between suppliers, so that suppliers with a quality management system approved under ISO 9000 were subject to substantially less scrutiny than those who did not. In consequence, deliveries of coil are normally accepted on the basis of the supplier's ISO 9000 approval or a declaration/Certificate of Conformity, and routine testing of the incoming coil by coil-coating companies is rare.

The clauses on manufacture in the seven Agrément Certificates examined show the same situation. By their nature, it is possible for deliveries of coil to contain hidden defects. All companies have complaint procedures which allow such events to be investigated with the supplier and one company explained that their practice is to isolate such material for examination during their supplier's regular technical service visit.

The arrangements for the supply of coil, the associated quality assurance and the rectification of complaints are greatly eased by the disciplined framework provided by the relevant British and European Standards for metal coil, which define both the technical properties and delivery requirements and are later described in detail in Tables 10 and 11.

Suppliers of coil coatings

Questionnaires were sent to ten manufacturers of coil coatings and five replies were received. Visits were made to six manufacturers.

The companies are all well established, well capitalised international companies, committed to research and development. Of the six companies investigated, five have a quality management system approved under ISO 9000 and the sixth is seeking this approval. There are no external standards for coil coatings (apart from PVF_2* paints which the companies produce under licence and where the original supplier exercises some control as a condition of the licence), so the products are produced to manufacturers' specifications.

The quality control conducted on the products varies between companies and products but the tests reported include solids content, specific gravity, viscosity, gloss, flash point, colour, adhesion, curing characteristics, fineness of grind and physical tests on the cured product. Some companies described their retained sample procedure (for liquid paint and coated panels) and the pre-delivery sample they provide for their customers. One company described the detailed investigation undertaken when a customer first uses the company's paint in production.

All the companies described the technical support they can offer to companies who use their products, and the separate survey of coil-coating companies confirms that these companies receive technical support from their suppliers on problems in production or in service.

Suppliers of pretreatment chemicals

Questionnaires were sent to five manufacturers of pretreatment chemicals; and three replies were received. A visit was made to one of these companies.

There are no relevant product standards for pretreatment chemicals and materials are produced to manufacturers' specifications. The product ranges available are comprehensive and cover all parts of the pretreatment cycle, all substrates in use and can be applied by a number of techniques. All three companies have quality management systems approved under ISO 9000 and carry out routine testing of all batches to ensure compliance with the product specifications.

Service visits are regularly made by suppliers to coating companies and additional technical visits are made as required to resolve any

---

*Throughout this report, PVF_2 is used as an abbreviation for polyvinylidene fluoride. PVDF is often used as an alternative abbreviation.

application problems. Laboratory facilities are available for sample analysis where necessary, although few coil-coating companies report difficulties with their pretreatment processes.

Coil coaters

Questionnaires were sent to twelve coil coaters, which included manufacturers from the UK, Europe and outside Europe, and a total of seven relevant replies were received. Visits were made to five companies.

Two separate manufacturing philosophies have been identified and are illustrated in Figure 2. As the manufacturer, the coil coater exercises complete control over the source and quality of all raw materials and markets the final product under a proprietary name. Alternatively, the coil coater may operate as a toll coater, where coil is supplied by a sponsor for coating with a particular coating and is returned to the sponsor for subsequent processing and marketing. This second procedure is widely carried out in the United States and it is believed that two companies in the UK operate in this way. Of the visits carried out, one was to a toll coater and the others to companies operating the more usual procedure.

All of the companies contacted have quality management systems approved under ISO 9000 or are seeking this approval. Some distinction can be made between the toll coaters and the other companies, in that the toll coater has no control over the source and quality of the coil being coated — this is the responsibility of the supplier. The toll coater visited described faults that the company is able to identify and report to customers and the tests which are conducted on the coated coil, but there is the possibility that inferior

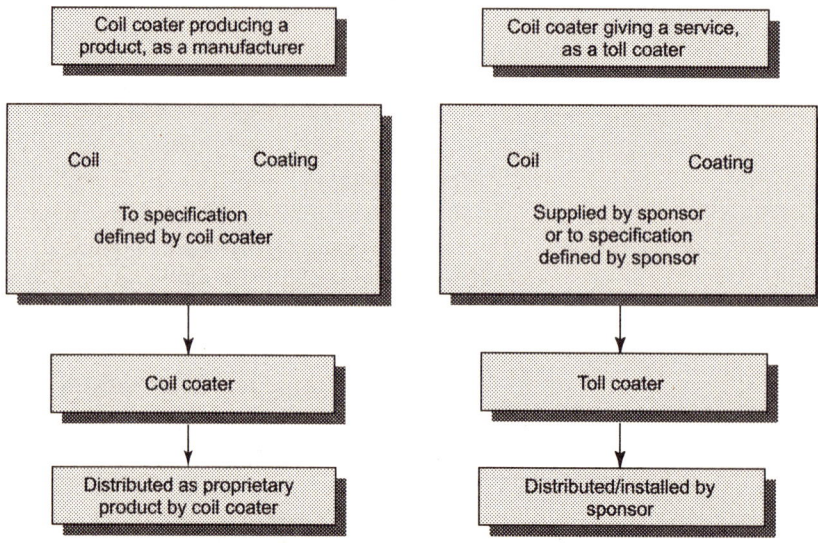

Figure 2. Distinction between roles of coil-coating companies

coil (outside British and European Standards which cover the properties of the coil in some detail) could enter the market by this route.

The control exercised by the coater over pretreatment and paint raw materials is limited, with emphasis for this again being placed on suppliers. Companies have procedures in place for the approval of suppliers and pre-delivery paint samples are commonly used to ensure acceptability prior to line use. Six survey replies reported lines over 1 m wide which are able to produce the width normally used as cladding and roofing, but the seventh (630 mm maximum) also has experience in cladding and roofing despite the narrow width produced. Line speeds were found to vary widely between companies. The companies described their testing — which included tests for colour, gloss, impact resistance, flexibility, adhesion, hardness, solvent resistance, coating thickness — but the exact procedures used differed between companies, with some properties being monitored in-line and others determined in final testing.

Of the seven companies who replied to the survey, four companies supply all their production to roll-forming companies, but three also roll form their product into profiles. Companies were asked for their experience of problems in service — the two who described problems in service also roll form their products. This tends to suggest that feedback on defects from independent roll-forming companies may be inadequate, but the separate survey conducted on roll-forming companies showed that their practice is to involve the supplier in appropriate complaint investigations as a matter of routine.

This topic was investigated further during the visits made to coil-coating companies. These companies all have technical staff available to investigate complaints and they involve their suppliers (the manufacturer of the coil coating) in the investigations when this is necessary. Coil coaters also reported that they often receive complaints on forming and installation, which are properly the concern of the roll-forming company or installer.

Two suppliers were found to be offering written guarantees on the performance of their coated steel products in service. As such, they offer the building owner/occupier a single point of contact for any future problems and eliminate the chain of responsibility that normally exists as a result of the multi-company method of production. These guarantees are issued to the registered owner and cover the external face of products against failure of the coating system for a given period, depending on the product used and its location. One UK roll former offers a similar guarantee for a coated product supplied by a European coil coater from the same company group. All three guarantees define a failure as the point at which greater than 5% of the paint is flaking on any surface of any single plane. All carry similar exclusions, which are not considered unreasonable, such as damage incurred during installation, unusually corrosive atmospheres, etc., and have requirements for regular maintenance. Previous studies have drawn attention to the incidence of corrosion at cut edges[3,16] and this remains a current concern. The three guarantees treat this type of failure differently — one excludes it from the guarantee; one specifically requires yearly inspection and maintenance of the cut edges; the third covers such corrosion where a given degree of peel back occurs within ten years. Cut edge corrosion is discussed further in Chapter 2 of this report.

Roll formers

Questionnaires were sent to sixteen companies and nine replies were received. Visits were made separately to eight companies.

The questionnaires asked the companies to describe their quality control arrangements. The nine companies who replied all have quality management systems approved under ISO 9000 and referred to the Quality Manual associated with this approval. The companies all conduct site visits in the case of complaints and four stated that their supplier would accompany them if it were appropriate.

The nature of the roofing industry makes it difficult for roll formers to influence the quality of installation of their products since the contractor may have a high turnover of on-site personnel, making training difficult. Of the roll formers contacted, all are prepared to train installers if asked to do so by the contractor, but none sell only to such companies — they all trade on the open market. One company does operate an approved applicator scheme where a controlled proportion of installers have been trained at the roll former's premises and specifiers are strongly recommended that these approved installers are employed. Two others have a recommended list of installers and a further two stated that visits can be made to installations in progress for on-site training where required. In general, companies who offer a proprietary system to their own design give detailed training in the particular techniques needed for their system, and companies who supply standard sheets which can be installed by standard methods anticipate that installers have the skills necessary to install these materials and thus do not offer specific training.

Concern over possible corrosion at end laps and the trend to install at lower pitches have led to an increasing use of long profile lengths, with products up to 45 m long being transported by road. The delivery of such lengths causes obvious difficulties in transport, delivery and handling and one alternative to such an approach is the roll forming of products on site. This process is common in Germany and the United States but has only been used by a small number of companies in the

UK. Some British companies have experienced difficulties in roll forming poor-quality coils and have rejected this approach, or consider that the tight quality control required for relatively sophisticated products such as secret-fix systems is more easily achieved in a factory environment.

Installers
A total of 679 questionnaires were sent to companies which were known to have knowledge of metal roofing or cladding installation. Their role in the work was not known and the survey asked the company to identify this (as specifier, installer or occupier). A total of 22 replies were received from installers and are considered in this section. The replies received from specifiers and occupiers are considered in Section 1.1.3.

The form did not enquire on formal quality procedures or on complaint procedures, but asked the companies to describe the length of their experience, the materials (substrates and coatings) used, the source of the materials, the location and nature of the buildings where they were used, and invited comments on problems in installation or service.

All respondents except one claimed a minimum of five years experience with the materials, and the variety of materials used and buildings quoted indicate that the replies received were from companies with substantial experience of the products. Few problems in installation were reported. The number of reports on performance in service are given in Table 5. Some replies stated the length of time before faults occurred, or gave a possible cause for the failure, or quantified the extent of the problem. None reported that such occurrences were widespread, and replies to other questions on the anticipated life of the installations or whether they would use the products again indicated that the companies were generally satisfied with the performance of the products.

1.1.3. Defects feedback from other sources

Questionnaire
The general questionnaire sent to installers also attracted 42 replies from specifiers, eleven from occupiers and three which could not be classified; the replies from specifiers, occupiers and unclassified are considered together in this section.

The replies received indicated the companies had experience of coated metal roofing and cladding on a regular basis, with a large majority having more than six years' experience of the materials, some with more than twenty years' experience.

The nature of the replies, with each respondent claiming knowledge of several materials in varied situations, confirmed the wide experience of the companies in the survey. The majority of the replies to questions about problems in installation or in service showed that problems had been experienced. The strongest comments received were made by a company with 15–20 years experience of specifying coated metal cladding and roofing who gave the following reply to a question on problems with installation

'Problems with lack of knowledge/care by "so-called" experienced specialist sub-contractor for *very* large cladding contract'

and to the question of whether they would use the materials again:

'Yes, but careful selection of specialist sub-contractors is vital (and difficult)'.

In general the levels of satisfaction reported and the anticipated life described in replies to other questions showed that the difficulties reported were not widespread, and that they indicated failure to achieve the potential properties of the products rather than any fundamental deficiency in their performance.

Feedback associated with Agrément Certificates
There are 29 current Agrément Certificates in the field of coated metals.[2] The BBA has a policy of investigating complaints it receives under its Certificates, is able to investigate the complaints record held by its Certificate holders during the routine factory visits it conducts, and conducts a formal review of its Certificates at three-year intervals. The complaints feedback from these sources is examined in this section.

The BBA set up a computer complaints database in November 1990 and all complaints received since that date are formally recorded and can be accessed by the BBA. The complaints logged on all products to date are listed in Table 6. The two coated metal complaints reported in Table 6 concern poor installation of a composite panel and gassing of a powder coating on galvanised steel.

Table 5. Summary of complaints received as reported by installers

Comment	Number of companies making comments
Cut edge corrosion	11
Coating delamination	11
Rooflight failure	8
Excessive colour loss	7
Fixings corrosion	5
Chalking	4
Other	8

Table 6. Summary of complaints received by the BBA since 1990 (from the BBA complaints database)

Total complaints on all Certificates (technical and commercial)	906
including technical complaints on all Certificates	130
Total technical complaints relating to roofing and cladding (all types) by product type:	
Fibre-reinforced cement and ceramic	9
Liquid applied	8
Membrane	3
PVC	2
Coated metal	2
Bitumen tile	1

Table 7. Summary of complaints recorded by Agrément Certificate holders for coated metals

Reports examined	53
No complaints recorded against product	37

Comments	Reports making comment
One reported complaint since previous visit	6
Supply and packaging complaints on powder coatings	2
Two reported complaints since previous visit	1
'Complaints not handled in accordance with defined procedures'	1
Complaints record could not be examined	1
Complaints record held elsewhere	1
'Several complaints' on cover width of formed profile	1
Chips in powder coating	1

A condition of any Agrément Certificate is that regular factory visits are conducted to the place of manufacture. Many of these visits are conducted by BSI Quality Assurance on the BBA's behalf and their reports regularly include a statement on the complaints which the Certificate holder has received and investigated through its own complaints procedure. Reports of factory visits made by BSI QA to holders of Agrément Certificates for coated metals were also examined and are summarised in Table 7.

The BBA's policy is to conduct a review of its Certificates every three years. In the review the BBA seeks direct comments from users of products in a user survey. Sixteen review reports conducted from 1990–1996 and covering coated metal Certificates were examined and the users' comments are given in Table 8.

Construction Quality Forum
The DOE Construction Sponsorship Directorate and Building Research Establishment operate a Construction Quality Forum. Its function is to promote better building by encouraging the exchange of information about failures and defects and it has established a database for failures to facilitate this.

A search was conducted for defects associated with metal sheeting and the results are shown in Table 9. The twelve reported failures in Table 9 represent eleven failures associated with design and installation and only one associated with materials.

The Construction Quality Forum's procedures are to conduct workshops in subject areas which cause concern. The level of failure reported on coated metal roofing and cladding is not considered sufficient to justify a workshop on the subject.

1.1.4. Guarantees offered by suppliers

Two UK manufacturers of coated steel sheet and one UK roll-forming company which supplies profiled coated steel sheet offer guarantees on installations in the British Isles.[17-19] These companies offer guarantees

Table 8. Analysis of performance of coated metals reported to the BBA during routine reviews of Agrément Certificates

Number of survey forms distributed	Replies received	Satisfaction reported	Nature of complaint	Nature of product
11	4	2	1 microcracking at bend 1 paint starvation	Coated aluminium
20	12	9	2 flashings 1 packaging	Aluminium roof system
22	16	14	1 deformation at clips 1 installation difficult in wind	Steel roof system
29	15	12	1 ease of damage 1 change of colour 1 directional nature of metallic finish	Coated steel
16	5	5		Coated steel
5	4	3	some application difficulties	Coating for metal
18	9	9		Coated aluminium
27	19	18	1 related to previous formulation	Coated steel
Not recorded	7	7		Aluminium roof system
10	3	3		Coated aluminium
5	1	1		Coated steel
28	12	12		Coated aluminium
21	17	17		Powder coating
19	10	10		Coating for metal
8	7	7		Aluminium roof system
54	26	20	4 application difficulties 1 corrosion of substrate 1 colour	Powder coating

Table 9. Summary of complaints recorded on Construction Quality Forum database

Total complaints on database	528
Complaints associated with metal sheeting	12
Nature of complaint:	3
movement related	3
ventilation problems	3
flashings	3
strength and stability	1
weathertightness	1
metal coating failure	1

on their products in respect of coating adhesion, but not colour stability. The period guaranteed varies between products and may be linked to the location of the building, the position of the product in the building and, in some cases, to the colour used and the orientation of the building. The guarantees are offered for installations in the British Isles and are not offered for other locations. The guarantees issued against these procedures identify the products used and define the installation under guarantee. They record the sheeting contractor and profile manufacturer and may record the main contractor or architect.

All guarantees require a certain level of failure to be reached before remedial action will be taken. They relate to the external face only and recognise cut edges as a cause of failure, but differ in how they approach this subject. Broadly, they have similar exclusions, but these are often expressed in different terms. They anticipate that routine maintenance inspections are conducted and documented annually — recommendations which closely follow the ECCA's recommendations for maintenance.[9]

1.1.5. Standards for coil

Standards for coated steel and aluminium
There are current British and European Standards for uncoated steel and aluminium coil (i.e. the raw material which is coil coated). Standards for coil-coated steel and aluminium were adopted as BS ENs during 1997.

Commentary on standards for steel coil
The current published standards for steel coil are given in Table 10.

- Galvanised steel was previously covered by BS 2989[20] which gave the tensile and forming properties, coating mass and dimensional tolerances for both structural and non-structural grades.

COATED METAL ROOFING AND CLADDING

- EN 10142 now covers the tensile and forming requirements and coating mass for non-structural steels, and EN 10147 gives more detailed requirements for structural steels.
- EN 10143 gives the delivery requirements for both forms of galvanised steel (and is also appropriate for steel with alloy coatings).
- Together, EN 10142, 10143 and 10147 replace BS 2989 (and also replace the earlier Euronorms 142, 143, 147 and 148).[11]
- EN 10154 covers steel with an alloy coating of aluminium – silicon. This product was once on the market in the UK and was the subject of BS 6536,[21] but there are no current UK suppliers.
- EN 10214 covers steel with an alloy coating of zinc – aluminium (95:5). The coating carries the trade name Galfan and was developed by the International Lead Zinc Research Organisation, Liege. British Steel (Shotton) hold a licence to produce the product, but have not yet done so.
- EN 10215 covers steel with an alloy coating of aluminium – zinc (55:33.4:1.6 Al:Zn:Si). The coated product carries the trade names of Zalutite, Galvalume or Aluzinc, and was previously covered by BS 6830.
- EN 10214 and 10215 cover the tensile and forming requirements and coating mass for both structural and non-structural steels. The delivery requirements are covered by EN 10143.

Table 10. Current standards for steel coil

Steel	
BS EN 10020: 1991	Definition and classification of grades of steel
BS EN 10021: 1993	General technical delivery requirements for steel and iron products
Galvanised steel	
BS EN 10142: 1991	Specification for continuously hot-dip zinc-coated low carbon steel sheet and strip for cold forming — technical delivery conditions
BS EN 10143: 1993	Continuously hot-dip metal coated steel sheet and strip — tolerances on dimensions and shape
BS EN 10147: 1992	Continuously hot-dip zinc coated structural steel sheet and strip — technical delivery conditions
Aluminium alloy coated steel	
BS EN 10154: 1996	Continuously hot-dip aluminium – silicon (AS) coated steel strip and sheet — technical delivery conditions (this EN replaces BS 6536: 1985 which implemented Euronorm 154 as a British Standard)
Zinc–aluminium alloy coated steel	
BS EN 10214: 1995	Continuously hot-dip zinc – aluminium (ZA) coated steel sheet and strip — technical delivery conditions
BS EN 10215: 1995	Continuously hot-dip aluminium – zinc (AZ) coated steel sheet and strip — technical delivery conditions
Inspection documents (appropriate for all metals)	
BS EN 10204: 1991	Metallic products — types of inspection documents

Table 11. Current standards for aluminium coil

Aluminium	
BS EN 485	Aluminium and aluminium alloys — sheet, strip and plate
BS EN 485-1: 1994	Part 1. Technical conditions for inspection and delivery
BS EN 485-2: 1995	Part 2. Mechanical properties
BS EN 485-4: 1994	Part 4. Tolerances on shape and dimensions for cold-rolled products
BS EN 515: 1993	Aluminium and aluminium alloys, wrought products — temper designations
BS EN 573	Aluminium and aluminium alloys — chemical composition and form of wrought products
BS EN 573-1: 1995	Part 1. Numerical designation system
BS EN 573-2: 1995	Part 2. Chemical symbol based designation system
BS EN 573-3: 1995	Part 3. Chemical composition
BS EN 573-4: 1995	Part 4. Forms of products

Inspection documents (appropriate for all metals)	
BS EN 10204: 1991	Metallic products — types of inspection documents

All the standards for steel described above include a designation which enables the grade used to be described unambiguously, and define the information which the purchaser should provide for the manufacturer. The latter includes the level of inspection and documentation which the purchaser requires of the manufacturer — levels which are described in EN 10204.

Commentary on standards for aluminium coil
The current published standards for aluminium coil are given in Table 11.

Aluminium sheet and coil was previously covered by BS 1470[22] which has been superseded by the European Standards quoted above. In these standards, EN 573-1 describes the International Designation System for Wrought Aluminium Alloys of the Aluminium Association,[23] which was previously used in BS 1470 : 1987; EN 573-2 describes the notation for alloys based on their chemical content which was used in ISO 209[24] and which can be used to supplement the numerical designation of EN 573-1; and EN 573-3 gives the limits for chemical composition appropriate to these designations. EN 573-4 indicates the form in which the alloys are available; among the alloys listed available as sheet are 1070, 3003, 3004, 3005, 3105 and 5251, which have an established history of use for cladding and roofing.

EN 485-1 describes the requirements on the coils' properties and documentation which the purchaser of the coil (the coil coater) should provide for the manufacturer. It refers to chemical tests to confirm compliance with EN 573-3, mechanical tests to confirm compliance with EN 485-2 (which gives the appropriate properties for particular alloys to EN 573-1 and particular tempers to EN 515), dimensional tests to confirm compliance with EN 485-4, and inspection and documentation in accordance with EN 10204.

Standards in preparation (for coated coil)
There are no published British or European Standards for organically coated metal coil or sheet specific for use in building. The standards in the course of preparation are given in Table 12.

The separate parts of pr EN 508 all include definitions, basic material and structural requirements, some details of test methods and information on marking, labelling and packaging for roofing sheets made from the three metals. pr EN 10169-2 covers coated steel and gives approved substrates and performance requirements for the coatings and coated products, details of inspection, sampling, marking, packaging, despatch and storage.

EN 1396 covers aluminium and gives definitions, technical conditions for inspection and delivery, mechanical properties, organic coating properties, inspection documents, with details of test methods and requirements where appropriate. In common with EN 10169-1 (but unlike pr EN 10169-2) this standard is not specific to exterior building applications.

1.1.6. Analysis — coil-coated metals roll formed into conventional profiles

The sequence of operations from the manufacture to installation of coil-coated roll-formed metals was shown in Figure 1. There is some vertical integration in the process — some metal companies may conduct coil coating and may control roll forming and installation companies, but this integration is in no way complete.

Table 12. Proposed standards for coated coil

pr EN 508	Roofing products from metal sheet — specification for self-supporting products of steel, aluminium and stainless steel
pr EN 508-1	Part 1: Steel
pr EN 508-2	Part 2: Aluminium
pr EN 508-3	Part 3: Stainless steel
EN 1396	Aluminium and aluminium alloys — coil-coated sheet and strip for general applications — specifications
EN 10169	Continuously organic coated (coil-coated) steel flat products **Note:** This subject was previously covered by BS 6781: 1986[25] which implemented Euronorm 169 as a British Standard, but covered all uses for the product and was not restricted to building applications.
EN 10169-1	Part 1: General information (definitions, materials, tolerances, test methods)
pr EN 10169-2	Part 2: Products for building exterior applications

The response to failure, customer service and compliance with standards described in this section are generally handled in two ways. They show a pattern of good practice which is widespread but not universal, with good cooperation between the different parties to the work, which offers traceability of materials back to their origin, a variety of materials with a well established history of satisfactory performance in use, and guarantees on materials and workmanship. The circumstances which prevent this situation being achieved regularly and with certainty are explored in Section 1.2 and recommendations are made to foster the good practice described and to close the gaps which have been identified.

Suppliers of metal coil produce coil to national or European Standards, under management systems approved under ISO 9000, and they have well established complaints procedures which work satisfactorily. They give technical service to their customers, the coil-coating companies, which largely concerns problems in production, but they are prepared to investigate failures in service where these relate to the base metal.

Manufacturers of coil coatings are well established international companies which are committed to research and development. They have good relations with polymer suppliers and may conduct collaborative work with them, but the initiative for development work and the responsibility for performance in service rest almost exclusively with the coil coating manufacturer. The companies have management systems approved under ISO 9000 (and one company is seeking this approval). There are no product standards for coil coatings but the companies' development procedures are such that new products are given realistic trials before they are marketed, and the supplier of PVF_2 resins operates some control as a condition of the licence granted to the companies to produce PVF_2 paints. The companies offer technical service to their customers, both on production problems and problems in service, and there is regular collaboration between them on new developments. The companies have an effective complaints procedure, which is assisted by the companies' routine use of retained samples of liquid paints and coated panels.

Manufacturers of pretreatment chemicals have comprehensive ranges of products and have procedures approved under ISO 9000. There are no product standards for pretreatment chemicals, but their composition is controlled to the manufacturers' specifications. The companies make regular service visits to their customers and have the facilities to investigate problems, but such investigations are seldom necessary.

Coil coaters are committed to ISO 9000, are members of the ECCA, and produce a range of products. European Standards have been prepared for coil-coated metal sheet and are about to be adopted as British Standards. Other standards are in the course of preparation and many products are already the subject of Agrément Certificates. Coil coaters have a close relationship with their suppliers and involve them in complaint investigations arising from production or failure in service as necessary. Coil coaters also offer technical service to their customer, the roll-forming company, and in some cases the roll-forming company may be controlled by the coil coater or they may both be members of the same group. Beyond the roll-forming company the coil coater offers technical service to the ultimate customer, the installer, and the owner/occupant of the clad building. The service they offer includes investigation of complaints, participation in MCRMA latent defects insurance or the NFRC Co-partnership Insurance Guarantee and some manufacturers offer a product guarantee.

Roll-forming companies who are members of the MCRMA are responsible for a claimed 85% of the UK market, are committed to ISO 9000, and seek it from their suppliers. Certain profiles are defined in British Standards and Codes of Practice, but a more detailed and current set of requirements on tolerances is given in the MCRMA publication *Manufacturing Tolerances for Profiled Metal Roof and Wall Cladding*,[13] which member companies observe. The companies offer technical service to their customers, which includes the cooperation of their supplier on complaints which involve the material supplied. They offer latent defects insurance through the MCRMA's arrangements,[13] and may participate in the NFRC's Co–partnership Guarantee, or the guarantee offered by their supplier.[17–19]

Installers who are members of the NFRC are committed to a Code of Conduct, which commits them to follow relevant Codes of Practice, use products complying with relevant standards, and to employ trained operatives. The NFRC has produced the *Guide to Good Practice for Profiled Metal Sheet Roofing and Cladding*, which members follow, and cooperated on the revision of BS 5427: Performance and Loading Criteria for Profiled Sheeting in Building. Members are obliged to inspect new work and rectify it if necessary, and to follow a disputes procedure. The NFRC offers a Co-Partnership Insurance Guarantee, and the supplier of the coated metal sheet (or the merchant supplying it) may be involved in the Guarantee through their associate membership of the NFRC.

One large roofing contractor, which operates nationally and cooperated during this investigation, has a quality management system approved under ISO 9000, but is not a member of the NFRC. The company's procedures enable non-conforming material to be traced back to the supplier, guarantees offered by suppliers are used, and this firm is an approved contractor for a standing-seam system. These arrangements are considered to offer an equivalent assurance to the arrangements operated by the NFRC.

The Confederation of Roofing Contractors operate substantially the same procedures and disciplines for their membership as the NFRC. Their arrangements are also considered to offer an equivalent assurance to those of the NFRC.

Specifiers and building owners who responded to the questionnaire described in Section 1.1.2 and detailed in Appendix 2 included many with some experience of failure, but this was not their regular experience and they continue to specify the materials. In general it is concluded that the materials can be installed to give satisfactory service, but this statement has wider implications which are explored in more detail in Section 1.2.

The evidence for failures reported to the BBA directly as complaints against certified products, through its review procedure on Certificates, and through its examination of complaints records held by the manufacturer during routine factory visits, and the evidence for failure experienced by the Building Research Establishment's Construction Quality Forum are small.

Quality Assurance systems are in place for coated metal roofing and cladding, good feedback arrangements exist and reported problems are rare. It is concluded that coated metal roofing and cladding currently on the market are capable of giving satisfactory service and that this is normally achieved.

1.1.7. Analysis — other materials and techniques

Section 1.1.6 considered the coil-coated product, roll formed into conventional profiles. Other materials and techniques are:

(a) secret-fix systems, roll formed from coated coil or mill-finish aluminium with a longitudinal seam characteristic of the particular system

(b) composite panels, with a coated metal facing and an insulating core

(c) preformed metal tiles, where coil-coated metal is pressed into a shape which simulates the appearance of a conventional tile or slate roof, or where the metal sheet is first formed and then coated

(d) powder-coated cladding panels of aluminium or galvanised steel

(e) laminates, produced from film in a coil-coating process and roll formed into profiles

(f) chipboard panels with a soft metal facing, for installation using traditional jointing techniques for soft metals.

The sequence of operations for these products is substantially the same as that for conventional profiles of coil-coated metals and is shown in Figure 3.

Despite the differences in detail there is at least the same measure of control and approval under ISO 9000 for these materials as there is for the coil-coated product, roll formed into conventional trapezoidal profiles. In the case of secret-fix systems the manufacturer exercises tighter control over application companies, and may restrict the use of the system to those companies who have received training in the appropriate techniques necessary for the particular system.

1.2. Gaps in approval systems

1.2.1. Weaknesses in procedures in the supply chain

Section 1.1.6 describes a pattern of good practice for coil-coated roll-formed metals. The circumstances which may prevent satisfactory performance being achieved regularly, with certainty, are explored in this section.

The specialist nature of some of the materials and techniques described in Section 1.1.7 results in a greater degree of control being exercised on companies installing them, and the reported level of failure is low. No specific weaknesses in approval arrangements can be identified for these materials, but the general weaknesses in procedure identified in this section could also apply to these materials. An expanded form of the distribution chain is given in Figure 4, and the possible weaknesses for each part of the operation are identified.

Steel and aluminium coil are covered by the standards described in Tables 10 and 11. However, the European Standards for galvanised steel include a variety of coating thicknesses and there is no obligation on the coil coater to use any particular coating thickness. A low coating weight specification could still be coil coated satisfactorily, but

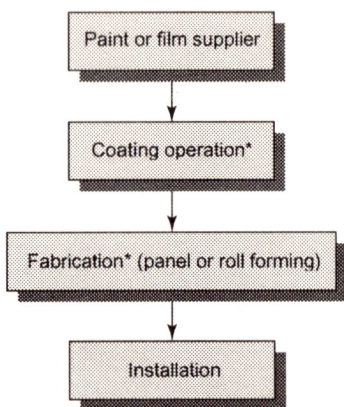

Figure 3. Supply chain for other products (not coil coated, conventional profiles)

*In the case of powder coating the operations indicated with an asterisk are reversed and the coating operation and materials are the subject of current British Standards BS 6496 and BS 6497. In the case of metal tiles these operations may be reversed.

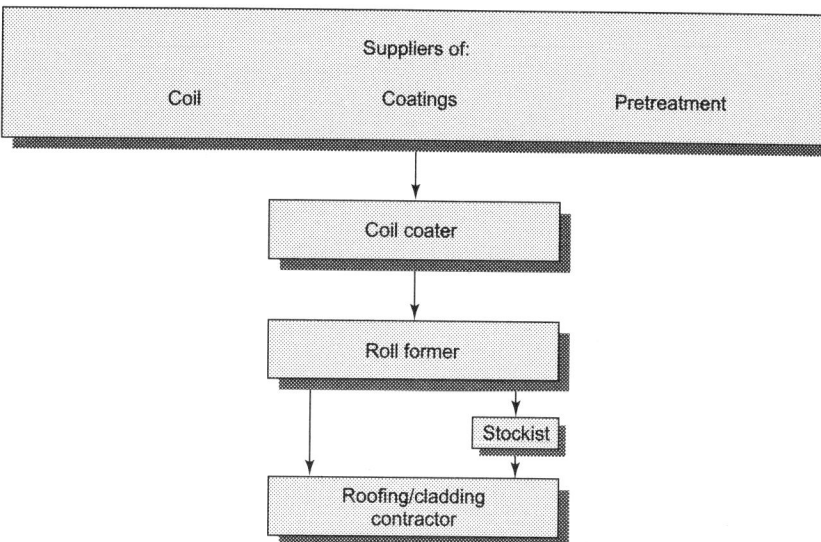

Figure 4. Potential weaknesses in supply chain for coil-coated roll-formed products

would be more at risk from corrosion in service. Similarly, the standards include a number of steel types, which may have inferior formability, but the use of these materials is considered less likely.

ISO 3575 is broadly equivalent to EN 10142, and imported steel to that standard (provided the same consideration is given to steel type and coating weight) can be considered equivalent to steel of European origin.

The European Standards for aluminium–zinc alloy coated steel include a variety of coating thicknesses, which lead to the same possibility of low coating weight material being coil coated and suffering premature corrosion described for galvanised steel above. The European Standards for aluminium define a variety of aluminium alloys, and there is no obligation on the coil coater to use any particular alloy. Alloys differ in their response to atmospheric exposure, and it is possible to coil coat some alloys satisfactorily, but for them to be more at risk from corrosion in service.

Coil coatings are not the subject of any particular standard and the less durable coatings have a variety of suppliers, and can be considered more a 'commodity' than a 'specification material'. There is thus the possibility of 'switching' between suppliers, with the risk that product quality could suffer.

Pretreatment chemicals are manufactured and supplied under good control and no potential abuses have been identified.

Coil coaters may operate in two different ways, as shown in Figure 2. Two different situations can be identified. The coil coater may produce a product to his own specification and market it as his product, or may operate as a toll coater who conducts coil coating as a service, to produce a customised product to the customer's specification. Both types of company have freedom of supply for coatings and coil as described above, but a particular concern is that a customer of a toll coater (which could be a roll-forming company or an installer) could deliberately commission a low-quality material.

Roll formers may be members of the MCRMA, who claim their members control 85% of the UK market, but roll forming can be conducted relatively easily, with modest capital outlay, and many other companies are able to roll form coil (but not in the same widths and volumes as the larger companies). These companies have freedom of supply, are not restricted to ISO 9000 approved suppliers as MCRMA members are, and are not obliged to produce profiles to the same tolerances as MCRMA members. There is thus the possibility for sub-standard materials formed to inaccurate tolerances to reach the market by this route.

Stockists take part in the distribution chain where the installer is not supplied directly from the roll former. Stockists can hold their own approval under ISO 9002 (from BSI or UK CARES), and two stockists of profiled metal sheet are Associate Members of the NFRC. BSI register stockists as Registered Firms with two levels of registration: level i 'Supplied from Quality Assured sources with lot traceability' or level ii 'Supplied from Quality Assured Sources (without lot traceability)'.[26] Stockists have a minor role in the overall chain from manufacture to installation, but their presence introduces the possibility that the traceability of the material used could be lost. To avoid this it is recommended that stockists should be approved under ISO 9002, and should meet level i requirements, which include 'lot traceability'.

Roofing/cladding contractors may be members of trade associations, the NFRC or CRC. It is estimated that there are 20 roofing contractors outside the associations for every member company. If the same proportion applies to metal roofing and cladding work there could be 4000 companies engaged in this work, or it could also be conducted by major building contractors. The design and installation of coated metal roofing and cladding is covered by various codes and standards which are reviewed in detail in Chapter 4 (for this analysis it is sufficient that such guidance exists).

The practice which roll-forming companies describe is that suppliers of specialist systems offer training to cover the specialist features of their system, and such companies offer 'approved contractor' status to the companies whose operatives they have trained, but the mainstream manufacturers of trapezoidal profiles do not provide such training and expect that operatives in the industry will necessarily possess the necessary skills. These mainstream manufacturers appear to be constrained by fair trading legislation. While they may wish to grant 'approved contractor' status on technical grounds to companies which they know to be competent and with trained employees, they consider they are unable to do so under fair trading legislation. (The issues of training, partnership and approval are considered in detail in Section 1.3.)

Concerns expressed in the survey from some respondents were that the poorest examples of workmanship had been seen on the largest sites and that installation companies with normally good records were still capable of producing sub-standard work if they recruited a poorly trained team.

1.3. The Latham Report[27] — recommendations relevant to the roof sheeting and cladding industry

This review was undertaken by Sir Michael Latham and culminated in his report *Constructing the Team*, published in July 1994.

1.3.1. Workmanship on site

Material producers and specialist contractors are acutely aware that good products can be spoilt by bad installation. This in turn can lead to disappointing performance from the point of view of durability in terms of weathertightness and appearance. In particular, the treatment of cut edges, flashings and the installation of rooflights were identified as sources of potential problems which can be exacerbated when untrained or incompetent labour is employed.

Normal practice is to retain a small core of key operatives whilst the large bulk of labour is recruited from unskilled casual sources on a site by site basis. The very young are often identified as unsuitable candidates purely on the grounds of their lack of developed physical strength and their possible irresponsibility whilst working on high and potentially dangerous parts of a building. Although this situation is not entirely unique to roofers and sheeters, it presents potentially severe problems because of the nature of the trade.

A widely held view of firms in this field is that the currently tight trading conditions do not allow them to release operatives from productive work to attend training courses. It is also clear from the CITB figures reproduced in Table 13 that the number of new entrants into the roof sheeting and cladding sector is dismally low.

COATED METAL ROOFING AND CLADDING

1.3.2. Latham recommendations

The Latham Report touched on two of the contributing factors to the above situations:

(a) unfair contractual conditions leading to poor margins and hence no 'slack' for the training of employees or the employment of newly trained and qualified tradesmen

(b) shortcomings in the training of new entrants and the updating of the existing workforce.

Extracts from the executive summary of *Constructing the Team* are given in Table 14.

It is not within the scope of this report to examine the wider non-technical issues relating to contractual and related matters above, except to point out that a better organised construction industry where profit margins were more realistic would give scope for the creation of a better trained workforce and, hence, lessen the occurrence of faults caused by poor workmanship.

1.3.3. *Training the Team*[28] — Report of Construction Industry Board (CIB) Working Group 6

The report of Working Group 6 (WG6), one of twelve such teams established to implement specific recommendations from the Latham Report, contains several points which are directly relevant to the training of roof sheeting and cladding operatives.

(a) Funding policy must be seen to protect the interest of minority trades in particular.

(b) There is undue emphasis on the acquisition of qualifications rather than the quality and breadth of training.

(c) The continuing economic climate will place added emphasis on the importance of the Industry Training Organisations (ITOs) in construction. Their principal tasks will be to ensure that

Table 13. *Extracts from CITB statistics for intake into Youth New Entrant Training Programmes*

Occupation	Trainees commencing course	
	1993/94	1994/95
All occupations	8304	9178
Building (all main trades, e.g. bricklaying, carpentry, plastering, etc.)	6964	7513
Specialist building (e.g. asphalting, tiling, floorlaying, felt roofing, glazing, etc. and *including roof sheeting and cladding*)	480	520
Roof sheeting and cladding	8	12

Table 14. Extracts from the executive summary of the Latham Report 'Constructing the Team'

15.   A list of contractors and subcontractors seeking public sector work should be maintained by DOE. It should develop into a quality register of approved firms (Chapter 6, paragraph 6.24). The proposed industry accreditation scheme for operatives should also be supported by the DOE (Chapter 7, paragraph 7.10).

18.   A joint Code of Practice for the Selection of Subcontractors should be drawn up which would include commitments to short tender lists, fair tendering procedures and teamwork on site (Chapter 6, paragraph 6.41).

19.   Recent proposals relating to the work of the Construction Industry Training Board (CITB) need urgent examination (Chapter 7, paragraph 7.25).

appropriate mechanisms exist for the promotion, delivery and funding of training to bridge the gaps between the training needs of employees individually and the training needs of the industry as a whole as perceived through improved manpower planning and to offset the adverse effects of economic cycles to which the industry is particularly vulnerable.

(d) The industry faces particular problems with regard to training for specialist trades which tends to be expensive as it caters for relatively low numbers but has to be available on a national basis. This must be given greater priority by local Enterprise Councils and ITOs in their current overall training strategies. Current pressures on colleges to adopt a commercial approach to their own funding is working against the construction industry where small classes using large floor areas for practical training are looked on as an uneconomic use of resources.

The last point has particular relevance to the needs of roof sheeting and cladding installer training.

WG6 emphasises the need for NVQs to become universally accepted and for the assessment methods used to gain the full confidence of the industry.

Support is also given to the concept of modern apprenticeships although greater direction from the Department of Education and Employment (DEE) is called for. In referring to 'site experience', WG6 points out that provision of appropriate work experience or on-the-job training is one of the main problems facing ITOs. The future of the current dual system requiring training periods both on-site and in college is threatened unless sufficient on-the-job training places can be provided. The safety requirements and type of manpower required on roofing, cladding and sheeting jobs does not lend itself readily to providing such places. WG6 is in favour of the Construction Skills Certification Scheme (CSCS) and it is believed that this is the only way the issues of training for self-employment can be resolved.

1.3.4. The Construction Industry Training Board (CITB) and the Direct Training Unit (DTU)

WG6 favours the retention of the CITB levy as a much needed stabilising factor in dealing with the vagaries of funding policy across building and civil engineering on a national basis. The CITB have also now introduced grants for new entrant trainees that can cover a three-year period to allow longer term planning by employers and continuity for trainees.

In 1996 the CITB's own DTU underwent major changes with roof sheeting and cladding courses being centred on the Birmingham and Glasgow training centres. However, the take-up of courses was very low with only five new entrants in Birmingham (to September 1996) and eight to ten in Glasgow. Qualification to NVQ Level 2 is offered. Only one part-time instructor covers both centres and he also services courses at colleges in Leeds and Bolton.

A more fruitful area is the provision of special three-day courses for firms and associations. For example, 153 operatives were trained under the auspices of MCRMA in 1993–1996.

Operatives with five years site experience can be given an updating course (strongly featuring safety) and then be assessed on-site by a general roofing instructor. This Accreditation of Prior Learning (APL) Scheme leads to a NVQ at Level 2. During 1995 the Birmingham DTU enrolled 67 and 50 passed. Approximately half were sheeters. However, the DEE cut back funding for APLs in 1996 and as of 1997 only 50 can be taken on the course.

1.3.5. Training by manufacturers of specialist systems

Some manufacturers of specialist systems, including secret-fix products, limit installation to firms whose site operatives have undergone product training. This is usually because the system has features which require special knowledge/skills to ensure a satisfactory job.

Agrément Certificates recognise this need and they clearly set out the requirements under the 'Installation' section of the Certificate. A typical paragraph reads:

> The roof system, including panels, panel splices, panel end closures, ridge and covers, gutter supports and gable fascias, is installed by specialist construction teams approved and trained by .... Ltd, generally working in accordance with the referenced installation manual.

The Agrément Certificate is only valid when systems are installed by approved contactors.

1.4. Conclusions

Section 1.1 recognises the good practice which already exists in the industry. Accordingly no direct recommendations are made on the supply of goods and services, but recommendations are made to encourage responsible specification by the specifier and client, and through this to create market pressure to foster the practices described in Section 1.1, and to discourage those described in Section 1.2.

Section 1.2 shows possible routes for base material with a low corrosion specification and for low-durability coatings and profiles with inaccurate tolerances to reach the market. If the material is considered a 'commodity' without any definite identity, there is scope for 'product switching', whereby the product installed may not have the identity or the performance expected. This section has also shown that poor standards of installation are possible.

The more detailed investigation in Section 1.3 has shown that many defects can be traced back to inexpert installation, often by operatives without any training whatsoever. It deduces that roof sheeting and cladding is one of the worst sectors in an industry generally bedevilled by a largely untrained and unregistered workforce, but that one exception is when installation of specialist systems is limited to approved (trained) installers. It is concluded that the Latham Report and the report of WG6 have made sound recommendations which deserve the widest support and, in particular, attention is drawn to the need to encourage more interest in the training of new entrants into this specialised field and the adoption of the CSCS (Construction Skills Certification Scheme).

1.5. Recommendations

It is recommended that:

(a) Specifiers and clients should:
   (i) specify materials to be used unambiguously, so that product switching to an inferior material is not possible. Current aids to specification are Agrément Certificates and established formulations from suppliers with ISO 9000 approvals and European Standards.
   (ii) use available guidance on design and specify appropriate methods for installation (for example BS 5427: 1996,[29] the

NFRC Guide to Good Practice,[14] specific guidance relating to the product from its supplier, or the appropriate MCRMA Design Guide[13]

(iii) ensure that the installer takes part in the insurance and guarantee arrangements which exist through the supplier or through trade associations, and ensure that the contract is covered by the guarantee and insurance which are available

(iv) ensure that the material used is the material specified (the products of the major roll-forming companies are branded to make this possible) and is traceable back to its origin through ISO 9000 procedures along the supply chain

(v) recognise that annual inspection and maintenance is necessary for installations and establish this procedure following ECCA's recommendations[9] or specific recommendations made by the supplier (which may be a condition of the supplier's guarantee).

(b) Recommendations made in the Latham Report and by Working Group 6 on the cladding and roofing industry should be supported, and in particular those to encourage the training of new entrants into the industry by the adoption of the Construction Skills Certification Scheme.

2. Trends in materials and techniques

The first British Standard to give general guidance on the use of coated metal in trapezoidal profiles for roofing and cladding was BS 5427: 1976.[30] This chapter describes the developments which have taken place in coatings, techniques and metals since 1976, and compares them with the products and techniques described in the standard.

2.1. Trends in coatings

2.1.1. Review of changes since 1976

There is a long-standing history of use in the UK of plastisol-coated steel and PVF_2-coated aluminium. Silicone–polyester and polyester coatings have been used on both metals and continue to be used, but in lower volumes, often in specialist markets such as the caravan industry. British Steel previously manufactured PVF_2-coated steel only for export markets but began marketing it in the UK in 1983.

The range of coatings available in the UK market in 1976 is described in Appendix E of BS 5427: 1976.[30] This guidance was reproduced in *Technical Guidance* by the Property Services Agency (which includes details of the suppliers of particular materials),[31] and by the European Convention for Constructional Steelwork in their *Good Practice in Steel Cladding and Roofing*.[10]

More recently ECISS and CEN have used this guidance as a basis for their own work, and have published it in revised form in current drafts and standards.[11,25,32–35] BSI have now revised the complete standard and have reissued it as BS 5427: 1996.[29]

The changes in the patterns of use of the coatings described in BS 5427: 1976 and the developments in coatings since that date are shown in Table 15, and the relationship between the coatings described in draft and current standards are shown in Table 16.

2.1.2. Developments in coil coatings

Plastisol
Plastisol-coated steel was originally produced in the UK by Richard Thomas and Baldwins at their Bryngwyn factory. After four years

Table 15. Current pattern of use of coatings described in BS 5427: 1976, PSA Technical Guidance* and ECCS Good Practice Recommendations

Surface finish described in BS 5427: 1976	Minimum thickness (µm) intended for		Surface finishes described in ECCS recommendations	Commercial relevance of finish in 1996.
	Aluminium	Galvanised steel		
Solution vinyl	20	20	Not included	Not seriously proposed for long-term external use by BS 5427: 1976. Not considered and not available in 1996.
Alkyds includes alkyd and oil-free polyester	20	20	Gives combined statement on polyesters and acrylics	Alkyds, polyesters and acrylics are all available. Alkyds tend to be used for other applications, or for the reverse side of sheet. Substantial Scandinavian experience with metallised amino-polyester. Polyesters and acrylics are used for roofing and claddings. Current costings favour the use of polyester.
Acrylics	20	20	Quotes three thicknesses, but only considers 25 µm for external exposure.	
PVC organosol	20	40	Not included	Not seriously proposed for long-term external use by BS 5427: 1976. Not considered for this use in 1996.
Silicone enamels includes silicone–acrylic silicone–alkyd silicone–polyester	20	20	Includes 25 µm silicone–acrylic and silicone–polyester	Used in UK but at relatively low volume. Wider use elsewhere in Europe and in export markets.
Fluoropolymers PVF and PVF$_2$ (liquid applied)	20	20	Includes 25 µm of PVF$_2$	PVF$_2$ is widely used on aluminium. Less substantial use on steel in UK, but wider use of PVF$_2$ on steel in export markets. PVF$_2$-coated stainless steel is now available.
Fluoropolymers PVF and PVF$_2$ (film applied)	20	35	Includes 50 µm of PVF	Available, but little use of fluorocarbon laminates in UK.
Vinasol	75	75	Not included	Impossible to trace any knowledge of material. Little guidance in BS 5427: 1976, not known since.
Plastisol	175	175	100–200 µm	Widely used on steel, at 200 µm thickness.
PVC film	175	200	100–250 µm	Available, but little use of PVC laminates in UK. Tend to be used for internal food-handling applications.
Acrylic film	50	70	85 µm	Acrylic film used for laminates in 1976; no longer available.
Polyester on asbestos–metal composite	100	100	Not included	Hot-melt polyester coating used on steel-epoxy resin composite since 1976; product no longer available.

*PSA *Technical Guidance* expands BS 5427 to include commercial details and profiles available, but does not introduce new materials or different thickness requirements.

development work the product was first marketed in 1965, and the decorative life then anticipated for the product was quoted as 15 years.

Since 1965, British Steel have expanded production to other sites, other suppliers (foreign steel companies and other UK coil coaters) have supplied plastisol-coated steel into the UK market, and substantial development on plastisols has taken place. This development has included detailed investigations on the product's durability which included the influence of colour, the local environment, orientation and the different performances achieved by roofing and cladding. British Steel responded to these developments by relaunching the product in 1979 and in 1986 (as HP200), and have linked their guarantee to the colour, location and orientation of the product.[17]

Substantially similar work has been conducted by other suppliers[19] and coil-coating companies and general advice on the durability of plastisols is given in Annex E of the draft European roofing standards for steel, pr EN 505[33] and 508-1.[35] More detailed guidance on the durability of plastisol is given in Annex D.5 of BS 5427: Part 1: 1996[29] (guidance which is not given for other coatings).

The commercial acceptability of PVC plastisols in future will inevitably be linked with the wider acceptability of the base polymer, PVC. There is a common perception that PVC is an environmentally unacceptable material, which has already affected the use of PVC in some markets and has prompted the development of alternative materials. This belief rests on a general distaste for all organic chlorine chemistry, and particular concerns expressed about PVC relate to the formation of dioxins during manufacture and incineration, the use of phthalate plasticisers in plasticised PVC,[37] in particular their perceived oestrogenic effect,[38] the presence of vinyl chloride monomer in PVC resin,[39] and the role of phthalate plasticisers in internal air quality.[40]

This general distaste is believed to be a response to particular issues raised by chlorine-containing chemicals such as chlorofluorocarbons, polychlorinated biphenyls, chlorine-containing insecticides and penta-chlorophenol. These compounds raise a variety of different issues which have been considered and resolved by the industries concerned, but it must be recognised that the compounds differ in composition from each other and from PVC, and that particular issues concerning particular compounds offer no rational basis for a generalised case against PVC.

The particular concerns against PVC have been addressed by producers and processors of PVC,[41-44] by the Health and Safety Executive,[45,46] and no concern over the use of PVC in construction is expressed in two green guides.[47,48] The implications of the oestrogenic properties of

Table 16. Coatings and thickness requirements described in current standards and drafts, compared with BS 5427: 1976

Finish	BS 5427: 1976		Coated metal standards [1]		Roofing standards [2]								BS 5427: 1996 [4]		Current code for coatings [5]
	Aluminium	Steel	EN 1396 Aluminium	pr EN 10169-2 Steel	EN 501 Zinc	pr EN 502 St. steel	pr EN 505 Steel	pr EN 506 Cu/Zn	pr EN 507 Aluminium	pr EN 508-1 Steel	pr EN 508-2 Aluminium	pr EN 508-3 St. steel	Aluminium	Steel	
Solution vinyl	20	20													PVC(S)
Alkyds	20	20	15	25–50	✓	25	✓	✓	√[3]	✓	✓	25	20	(20)	AK
Polyester	20	20	20				✓	✓	✓	✓	✓		20	20	SP
Acrylics	20	20	20	25	✓		✓	✓	✓	✓	✓		20	20	AY
Organosol	20	40													PVC(O)
Silicone–acrylic	20	20	20	25		25	✓	✓	✓	✓	✓	25	2C	20	AY-SI
alkyd	20	20													
polyester	20	20													SP SI
Fluoro-polymer liquid	20	20	20	25–60	✓	25	✓	✓	✓	✓	✓	25	20	20	PVDF
film	20	35	38	38			✓	✓	✓	✓	✓				PVF(F)
Vinasol	75	75													—
Plastisol	175	175		100–200	✓	80	✓	✓		✓		80	(200) [6] (100)	200 100	PVC(P)
PVC film	175	200	>100	200–800											PVC(F)
Acrylic film	50	70													PMMA(F)
Polyester composite	100	100													—

Coating				[8]√		√[7]			EP
Epoxy	5								
Polyamide / polyurethane / polyester	20 / 20	25		√	√	√ / √	20 / 20	(20) / (20)	PMD / PUR-PA / SP-PA
Polyurethane adhesive	6								PUR(A)
Polyurethane	20	25–60	25	√	√	√	25		PUR(A)
Chemical treatment			√		√				PW
Multicoat			√	√	√	√	(75)	75	—
PVDF polyurethane			√ [9]	√ [9]	√ [9]	√ [9]	(100)	100	—

Notes to Table 16

If standards make recommendations for the thickness of a particular coating, this is given in micrometres. If standards state a coating is suitable and available, without recommending a thickness, this is shown by √.

[1] BS 6781: 1986 EU169: 1985 (Euronorm 169),[25] now reissued as EN 10169-1[32] covers coated steel for all uses and gives a wide range of coatings and coating thicknesses not all of which are appropriate for building applications.

[2] pr EN 503 and 504[33] cover fully supported roofing of lead and copper and do not include any reference to coil coatings.

[3] The alkyd coating is only applied after fabrication.

[4] BS 5427: 1996 makes comments on whether particular coatings are available on the different substrates. Figures in parentheses indicate combinations which are considered technically acceptable but are not commercially available.

[5] The codes for coatings are described as corresponding to ISO 1043-1,[36] chosen by analogy, and include a suffix to show the form of the product.

[6] The standard distinguishes between an embossed surface with a 200 μm coating or a smooth or satin finish with a 100 μm coating.

[7] Restricted to use inside the building.

[8] The coatings described in other standards as polyamide-modified polyurethanes or polyesters are described in this standard as polyamide (PMD).

[9] The steel roofing standards also describe a multi-layer bitumen-based coating system, applied after manufacture. In UK practice products of this type are more commonly used for remedial reroofing for roof decks of other materials.

phthalates have been considered by Dr Sharpe,[49] and these are set in perspective by a recent study on natural products.[50]

It is concluded that there is no realistic technical or environmental case against PVC or plasticised PVC in current conditions of manufacture and use. Despite this, it is recognised that if these concerns come to be widely believed, the marketability and commercial use of plastisol-coated steel could be called into question.

PVF_2

Changes have taken place in the source of supply of PVF_2 resins for coil coatings, but no substantial change has taken place in these resins.

All coil-coating companies continue to supply a 70:30 PVF_2–acrylic paint, and one supplies the 85:15 product. Most PVF_2–acrylic paint is applied to aluminium, but British Steel began to produce PVF_2-coated steel for the UK market in 1983 (on galvanised steel or Zalutite) and H H Robertson began to produce a PVF_2-coated galvanised steel with an intermediate flexible epoxy resin basecoat in 1984. British Steel introduced a PVF_2-coated austenitic stainless steel in 1995.

These changes have been recognised in draft European Standards and in BS 5427: Part 1: 1996, as shown in Table 17.

Attempts have been made to formulate an abrasion-resistant PVF_2 coating, analogous to the successful abrasion-resistant polyamide-modified polyester/polyurethanes, but these developments have not been successful.

Polyesters

The standard polyesters and silicone–polyesters in use 20 years ago continue to be used for medium-life applications and polyesters are now preferred to acrylics in these applications. Substantial development work has been carried out on polyesters and a high-durability polyester coil coating, which differs substantially from standard polyesters in composition and performance,[51] has been developed and is in production.

Table 17. PVF_2 (PVDF) coatings in European and British Standards and drafts

	Metal standards		Fully supporting roofing			Self-supporting			BS 5427: Part 1: 1996	
	Aluminium EN 1396	Steel 10169-2	St. steel 502	Steel 505	Aluminium 507	Steel 508-1	Aluminium 508-2	St. steel 508-3	Aluminium	Steel
PVF_2 coating Multicoat	√	√	√	√	√	√	√	√	√	√
PVF_2				√		√			*	√

*Not available but the specification is considered acceptable.

Laminates

Little use is made of laminates (plastic film laminated to a metal coil in a coil-coating line) in the UK. The acrylic film available in 1976 and described in BS 5427: 1976 is no longer available. Current draft European Standards describe the use of PVF and PVC laminates but these see little use in roofing and cladding applications in the UK. (However, PVC laminate is preferred for internal use in food-handling applications,[52] vinyl film is used for advertising, graphics, etc.[53] and has been used experimentally in cladding applications,[54] and laminates are widely used in industrial applications.[55])

Abrasion-resistant systems

Polyurethane and polyester coatings incorporating a thermoplastic polyamide resin with a good resistance to scratching and abrasion were originally developed and used for transport applications (such as the back of bus seats). The external durability of these products was good and they began to be used for cladding and roofing in 1984. Agrément Certificates for the products allow them to be used in locations which are 'readily accessible to the public and to others with little incentive to exercise care', where there are 'chances of accidents occurring and of misuse', such as the 'walls adjacent to pedestrian thoroughfares or playing fields' away from vandal-prone areas.[56] Similarly, BS 5427: Part 1: 1996[29] acknowledges their abrasion-resistant properties.

The coatings are suitable for application to aluminium and to galvanised or aluminium–zinc alloy coated steel and this is recognised in BS 5427: Part 1: 1996 Appendix D.[29] To date they have only been used commercially on aluminium.

Polyurethanes

The coil-coating industry produces polyurethane coil coatings, but the dominant use of these in the UK is in industrial applications. Polyurethane coil coatings are included in pr ENs for steel, aluminium and roofing, and the use of high-build polyurethane systems is included in BS 5427: 1996[29] and pr ENs for steel roofing. The position of polyurethane coatings in the various standards is shown in Table 18.

Multicoat polyurethane on aluminium is not available commercially but 100 μm would be considered acceptable.

One manufacturer of coil coatings (Courtaulds Nippon Paint) lists high-build polyurethanes in its range of products.[57] In 1995 H H Robertson began to produce steel sheet with a polyurethane coil coating in two coating thickness specifications, and gave guarantees on the products' performance.[58] Armacor comprises 30 μm primer polyurethane top-coat on a 15 μm polyurethane primer (with a 5 μm primer and 10–12 μm polyester on the reverse) and has a 25-year guarantee. (The coating specification falls in to the range given in pr EN 10169-2 and has an embossed surface as described in the standard, but is not included in BS 5427: Part 1: 1996.) Versacor TF has a 40 μm polyurethane top-coat over a 65 μm coating of a flexible epoxy resin barrier coat* and primer (with barrier coat and polyester or polyurethane on the reverse) and has a 40-year guarantee. (The coating specification satisfies the descriptions in BS 5427: Part 1: 1996 and in the draft European standards for steel roofing.)

The potential for commercial use of polyurethanes does not rest entirely on the technical merits of the products, but is linked with the commercial acceptability of PVC. Although the environmental case against PVC is considered unfounded† there is a possibility that it could be heeded and a high-build polyurethane product has been developed to have properties and a price which would be acceptable to companies who habitually use plastisol-coated steel were it to become necessary for them to seek a suitable alternative.

2.1.3. Other developments

Powder coatings

Powder coatings are not used in building cladding to the same extent as the coil coated roll-formed products, but polyester powder coatings are used on preformed panels, designed for a particular application to achieve a particular architectural effect. The application and properties of powder coatings are covered by British Standards[60,61] Agrément Certificates (Appendix 1), and in current work by CEN TC 139 WG5 and WG8.[62]

Table 18. Polyurethane coatings in European and British Standards

| | Aluminium | Steel standards | | Fully supported roofing | | Self-supporting roofing | | | BS 5427: Part 1 1996 | |
	EN 1396	EN 10169-1	pr EN 10169-2	St. steel 502	Steel 505	Steel 508-1	Aluminium 508-2	St. steel 508-3	Aluminium	Steel
Polyurethane	20	10–60	25–60	25	√	√	√	25	—	—
Multicoat polyurethane	—	—	—	—	√	√	—	—	(100)	100

The table shows the coating thickness quoted in the standard in micrometres.
√ indicates a standard with no thickness requirement quoted.

*An epoxy resin barrier coat is used in Robertson's multicoat PVF$_2$ product, Versacor PF, and has been used on other Robertson products since 1975.[59] Before the epoxy resin barrier coat was developed H H Robertson used a bitumen – asbestos coating as an anti-corrosive barrier between the steel and the top-coat — a product which was described in BS 5427: 1976 but is no longer available.
†In the environmental debate PVC has attracted a depth of scrutiny that has not been applied to other materials, in particular to proposed alternatives. Without the same depth of investigation, claims on the environmental merits of alternative materials cannot be considered authoritative.

There have been developments in polyester powder coatings to improve their external durability, broadly in parallel with those in polyester coil coatings. Some of these developments have been directed to the motor industry[63] but are considered to have considerable potential for building applications, and some have been directly intended for use in building cladding.[64]

Changes have been made in the composition of polyester powder coatings to avoid the use of triglycidyl isocyanurate curing systems, to give a powder which can be handled more safely during application, and changes have also been made to reduce the products' curing temperature. The performance properties of the original material have been retained in the reformulations.[65]

A powder coil-coating process, where a powder coating is applied continuously in a coil-coating line, has been developed. A particular characteristic of this process is that the coating can be applied to a perforated sheet, to produce grilles, etc. but this property is more suited to other applications. There are powder coil-coating lines in Italy, France, the USA and England, and EN 10169-1 describes the use of powder coatings in a coil-coating line. Some Italian material has been imported, but there has been little commercial use of the powder coil-coated product in the UK. The line speed of the powder coil-coating lines currently in use in Europe is low, below the speed of conventional coil-coating lines, but SMS Schloemann-Siemag AG have recently taken up a licence to produce powder coil-coating lines with an intended line speed of 100 m/min.[66] This development is considered important and it is felt that any extensive use of powder coil-coated material can only take place once production becomes competitive.

Regardless of how they are applied — conventionally or in a powder coil-coating line — powder coatings are solvent-free and have a low emission of volatile organic compounds; hence they are acceptable under current environmental legislation and the proposed European solvents directive. The use of powder coatings is controlled in other respects under PG6/31.[67]

Epoxy powder coatings are available but have poor durability on external exposure and are restricted to concealed, internal and non-decorative applications. Sigma have produced a PVF_2 powder coating. There is experience of this product on aluminium cladding in Holland and Germany[68] and it is included in draft European standards for powder coating[62] but it has not been used to date in the UK. Other thermoplastic powder coatings exist, based on other polymers, but there is no history of use for these products on cladding.

Spray-applied fluoropolymer coatings

Besides manufacturing coil coatings, PPG Industries also supplies a PVF_2 – acrylic paint for application by spray in an industrial plant. The product is supplied as a primer, top-coat and clear glaze for a two or three coat application, and PPG restricts the use of the product to properly equipped application companies who operate an effective quality management system.[69] PPG primarily describes the product as for application to aluminium cladding panels and extrusions, but it is also applied to galvanised steel in a three-coat coil-coating operation (i.e. as a multicoat PVF_2 coating, as described in Table 15). There is over 20 years' American experience with this coating and 10 years experience in the UK. Its life is comparable to a PVF_2 – acrylic coil coating, and can be extended by applying a clear PVF_2 – acrylic top-coat. The product is also available in an air-drying form for application on site.

Croda Mebon produce a spray-applied urethane fluoropolymer coating, which is applied by spray in a two-coat application to galvanised steel or aluminium cladding panels, by competent spray contractors, either in the factory or on-site.[70]

More appropriate uses for spray-applied coatings are for extrusions, windows and structural steel, and relatively little (fluoropolymer or other systems) is used on cladding.

Corrosion protection applied by coil coating

There is a history of use in the motor industry of zinc/zinc phosphate in organic binders as coil coating for steel and the possibility of using such products in cladding and roofing was investigated in this study. There was no evidence in the industry of these products used for these purposes, no interest in doing so, and the motor industry has now largely introduced zinc/nickel electroplated coil for applications which once used these products.[71]

2.1.4. Health, safety and environmental issues

Chromium compounds

There is a long history of the use of chromate pretreatments of metals before industrial coating — British Standards for liquid applied coatings and powder coatings for aluminium require a chromate pretreatment[60] and the British Standard for powder-coated galvanised steel accepts chromate or phosphate as alternatives.[61] There is also a substantial history of use of chromates as corrosion-inhibiting pigments.

Chromium and its compounds are subject to occupational exposure limits which are defined by the Health and Safety Executive (HSE) and published in EH40 (which is revised annually).[72] There are a variety of

Table 19. Occupational exposure limits for chromium defined in EH40 — changes in requirements since 1984

| | Long-term exposure limit (8 h TWA* value, mg m^{-3}) | | | | | |
| | 1984–1988 | 1989–1992 | | 1993–1996 | | |
Nature of requirement	Recommended limit†	OES	Under review	OES	MEL
Chromium‡	0.5	0.5		0.5	
Chromium II	0.5	0.5		0.5	
Chromium III	0.5	0.5		0.5	
Chromium VI	0.05		0.05		0.05

*TWA-time weighted average.

†Prior to 1989, the occupational exposure limits published distinguished between control limits and recommended limits. The Control of Substances Hazardous to Health (COSHH) Regulations 1988,[75] which came into force in 1989, introduced maximum exposure limits (MELs) and occupational exposure standards (OESs).

‡The terms used in EH40 represent the limits for chromium metal, chromous compounds chromic compounds, and chromates respectively.

chromium compounds in difference states of oxidation (or valency) which differ in toxicity. Different limits are imposed on the different forms of chromium compounds and a tighter limit is imposed for chromates (hexavalent chromium or chromium VI). All occupational exposure limits may be subject to review as more evidence on the compounds becomes available — the limit for chromates was reviewed between 1989 and 1992 and the development of occupational exposure limits for chromium and its compounds (taken from EH40) is shown in Table 19.

The review was conducted by the Health and Safety Commission's Advisory Committee for Toxic Substances and the evidence before it was published in 1989.[73] This evidence commented on the high risk of skin sensitisation associated with chromates (which would be relevant for some metal finishing applications) and gave details of some industries where relatively high levels of exposure were experienced, but did not include metal finishing in the industries listed.

During the review, the HSE announced their intention to set a maximum exposure limit (MEL) for chromates in EH40 in 1991.[72] The maximum exposure limit (MEL) set was 0.05 mg m^{-3}, which retained the previous limit but tightened the nature of the requirement (from the previous occupational exposure standard (OES)). The basis for this change was published by the HSE in 1992,[74] and the review identified that the proposed limit was already being achieved regularly and concluded that the new 'limit will not result in significant extra burdens on industry'.

The Control of Substances Hazardous to Health (COSHH) Regulations and the associated Approved Codes of Practice were published in October 1988,[75] came into force in October 1989 and were revised in 1994.[76] The Regulations give greater emphasis to exposure limits (as described in Table 19), but also address chromium in other respects by including chromating in a list of processes where health surveillance of employees (skin inspection and retention of records) may be necessary (Approved Code of Practice, Regulation 11 cl 86/92[d] [i]) and by requiring insoluble chromium compounds (chromate pigments) to be labelled with the risk phrase 'R45: May cause cancer' (Approved Code of Practice for the control of carcinogenic substances 1988, Appendix 1).

Other factors which could affect the use of chromium in pretreatments are tighter requirements on chromates in effluent (water authorities impose limits of 1 ppm (1 mg/litre) or less for Cr^{6+} in effluent, have identified industrial sources as the origin of chromium in the water they supply[77], and are obliged to supply drinking water with a maximum chromium content of 50 μg/litre) and the fear that a chromate pretreatment on aluminium could hinder or prevent economic recycling. These factors have led to the development of chromium-free pretreatments (which are often targeted at parts of the metal-finishing industry with limited facilities for treating effluent) and the development of no-rinse treatments for coil coating (where the treatment reacts with the substrate on heating to give a coherent insoluble compound).[78,79]

Coil-coating manufacturers have developed primers containing alternative anti-corrosive pigments (other than chromates), but there has been little commercial use of these products. There are thus alternative products which could be used to replace (or in the case of no-rinse treatments, alleviate the perceived consequences of using) chromium compounds in pretreatments and primers. However, as the properties conferred by chromium are critical to the products' performance (and corrosion was identified as a problem in previous studies[3,16]), the proposed alternatives do not have the same history of use as chromate materials, and HSE publications[73,74] show that the limits now in force for chromium and its compounds can be easily achieved (and were being achieved when the limits were set), it is concluded that there is no realistic need for products to be formulated using chrome-free materials.

Restrictions on use of solvents
Volatile organic compounds (VOCs) are subject to occupational exposure limits,[72] and can contribute to poor internal air quality.[40] They can also take part in photochemical reactions, to create ozone at low levels in the atmosphere and destroy it at high levels.

An analysis of VOC emissions for the UK[80] showed that the industrial use of solvents in 1990 (including the use of coatings, adhesives and cleaning agents) represented half of all VOC emissions and that the level of emissions (1.2 million tonnes/year) had been relatively constant over 20 years. The UK signed a protocol under the UNECE Convention on Long Range Transboundary Air Pollution in November 1991, which required national VOC emissions to be reduced by 30% between 1988 and 1999.

In 1990 the controls on emissions from industrial plants which were previously controlled under the Health and Safety at Work Act came under the Environmental Protection Act. Part 1 of the Act required operators of prescribed industrial processes to obtain authorisation from local authorities and to prevent pollution by using 'best available techniques not entailing excessive cost' (BATNEEC). The prescribed processes included coil coating and powder coating, and appropriate operating techniques and control methods are described in guidance issued by the Secretary of State.[67] The guidance on coil coatings originally issued in 1991 has been reviewed, and was reissued in March 1997.[81b] The major changes are a revision of some emission limits, the extension of the deadline for existing plants to achieve compliance from October 1996 to October 1997, and the deletion of clause 51 from the original (which stated a preference for the use of water-based, high-solid, powder, solvent-free or radiation-curing coatings over incineration as ways of reducing VOC emissions). The deletion of this clause is a response to the coil-coating industry's experience. Latex systems have been available for some 20 years but experience in the UK has been disappointing — in particular they also contain VOCs and require a heat input to remove water with the result that any perceived environmental benefit they may confer in fact is illusory. Plastisol contains some 5–10% of solvent, so can be considered a high-solid or low-solvent content product, but the greater thickness of plastisol applied gives substantially the same VOC emission per unit area as other coil coatings applied at lower coating thicknesses. Radiation-curing systems are the subject of current research by the Paint Research Association[82] but this technique is believed to have more applications in other markets.

The European Commission envisaged making progress with a draft organic solvents Directive in 1996, but this is not expected to require more stringent standards than already exist in the UK.[83]

Powder coatings are 100% solids, are largely free from VOCs, and are applied in accordance with the Secretary of State's Guidance, which was originally issued in 1991 and has now been published in revised form.[67]

The constraints on VOCs also affect the use of solvent-based paints in other industrial processes and on-site. Alternative materials are being developed and water-based paints have been awarded an eco-label, but the use of solvent systems is still substantial. By avoiding the use of such products, there is an obvious environmental benefit in using a precoated material such as the coil-coated or powder-coated product, and this benefit should be recognised.

2.1.5. Corrosion prevention, maintenance and repair

Cut edge corrosion

Galvanised steel sheet has a facing of zinc on a steel core. At cut edges (i.e. at the edge of the sheet, damaged areas or penetrations) the steel core is exposed. In damp conditions the contact between steel, zinc and water creates an electrolytic cell, where the more reactive zinc dissolves, protecting the steel from corrosion. This process also takes place when the galvanised steel carries an organic coating. As the zinc is consumed, its ability to continue to protect the steel decreases, with the result that cut edges can eventually corrode. This effect is influenced by the position of the cut edge, the nature of the cut edge, the adhesion of any organic coating, the anti-corrosive properties of the primer, whether water can drain easily or is retained at the cut edge, and the general corrosive nature of the location it is in.

Previous studies have drawn attention to cut edge corrosion.[3,16] The perception is that this problem necessarily concerns plastisol-coated steel, but it can take place with any coated steel. Any emphasis given to plastisol is considered due to the long history of use of plastisol (with early applications now well past their proposed design life), and the high proportion of plastisol that has been installed.

Manufacturers' guarantees either exclude cut edge corrosion or require cut edges to be treated;[17-19] Annex E of the steel roofing standards pr EN 505 and 508-1 recommends either that cut edges of steel sheet used for roofing should be given additional edge protection or that the edge should be bent down to improve drainage, and Agrément Certificates for steel sheet recommend that cut edges of roofing sheets should be coated.

The experience of contractors is that the application of coatings to cut edges is laborious, tedious and difficult to conduct satisfactorily, and they have found that the operation may not be defined in specifications (i.e. not costed) but nonetheless may be expected of them. An alternative proposal — that the edges of a stack of sheared sheets could be coated by the forming company — is also considered unrealistic.

However, there are materials available for application to cut edges: either a latex system, which is colourless and can be applied to any colour sheet,[84] or a colour-matched product recommended by the supplier of the sheet, which can also be used to touch up damaged areas on the surface.[85]

An alternative strategy is to minimise the extent of sheet edges which are exposed. The techniques which can be used to achieve this are as follows.

(a)   To use a welted seam on flashings and at the edges of sheets. The effect of this is to ensure that there are no exposed edges on the external face of the installation, by removing the exposed edges to a more sheltered, concealed position away from the external face.

(b)   To use a secret-fix system or composite panels, which also ensure the exposed edges of sheets are concealed within the joint or away from the external face of the installation.

(c)   The installation of roofing sheet from eaves to ridge in a single operation, i.e. without lap joints (this technique has implications for site-handling and transport, but has been used successfully by companies with the necessary equipment and organisation).

Overcoating systems

Current manufacturers' literature and standards anticipate that cladding or roofing may be recoated, either to maintain high aesthetic standards or to extend the design life of the installation. For this work to be conducted economically it must be possible to apply any overcoating paint to large areas and the paint must be relatively unaffected by changes in site conditions.

Various manufacturers offer a one-pack moisture-curing polyurethane for this application, with detailed application specifications and different primers for use on the different coatings or the exposed metal surface.[86-88] The repainting work is normally conducted by specialist painting contractors. Should the coating have deteriorated sufficiently for corrosion of the metal to have taken place a separate system (described below) is available for this to be treated.

Remedial treatment of corroded areas

A silicone rubber based product for the remedial treatment of failed claddings and roofings has been developed. The product is available in colours formulated to match current cladding and roofing materials (but in weathered conditions). Weathered cladding/roofing are cleaned and corroded metal surfaces are grit blasted or ground back to clean metal and the coating is applied in a three-coat application, with a polyester fleece where reinforcement is necessary. A two-coat application is made on the side at eaves and gutters.[89] Application is restricted to the distributor's approved contractors and the specification for any proposed work is determined by a survey jointly conducted by the distributor and contractor. The manufacturer offers an eight-year guarantee on the system and a comparable silicone rubber product, used for a different roofing application, holds an Agrément Certificate which gives an anticipated minimum life of ten years.[90]

2.2. Trends in design

2.2.1. Review of changes since 1976

BS 5427: 1976[30] gives detailed text on roofing and cladding for simple structures with vertical walls and monopitched roofs with a minimum pitch of 10°. It describes some features which were not in widespread use in 1976 but have been developed further and have come into general use since that date. These techniques involve the use of curved sheets, ribbed profiles, composite panels, and secret-fix systems. These are all fully accepted and are now widely available and they are described in the current revision of BS 5427: 1996[29] and in guidance from the MCRMA[13] and EPIC.[91]

The development of these techniques and the acceptance they received is traced in Table 20.

2.2.2. Developments in design in profiled sheeting since 1976

Curved profiles
There is a long history of use of sinusoidally corrugated galvanised steel or aluminium in simple regular curved roofs or curved structures, and British Aluminium produced curved aluminium sheets, coated after forming. Since 1976 Ash and Lacy have introduced Floclad, a forming technique which forms a crimped curve in a trapezoidal profiled sheet of coated galvanised steel. This technique simulated a detail which could be achieved with asbestos cement (which could be produced in that shape) but was innovative for steel. It enabled a building to be built with no eaves detail, but with a continuous profiled curve between wall and roof. This technique has been widely adopted for steel and aluminium, and a wide variety of roll-formed and pressed sheets and flashings, smooth (i.e. crimp-free) curves, factory-assembled corners and tapered profiled sheets are now available (guidance on their use is given in MCRMA Technical Paper 2).[13] Innovation has continued and Hoogovens have designed and manufactured material for installation of curved tapered profiled sheet.

Ribbed profiles
The use of ribbed profiles enables a greater span to be achieved and the first reference to the product appears in Constrado's 1980 Guide. All manufacturers produce safe load–span tables, as required by BS 5427, to be used in structural calculations.

Composite panels
BS 5427 refers to 'laminated panels' and the PSA Technical Guides distinguish between laminated panels and composite panels where a rigid polymeric foam core is foamed between two metal skins. The Guides suggest the assembly can act as a composite, but warned that

local delamination between foam and skin was possible and that this should be investigated.

Constrado's 1980 Guide refers to composite panels being available from Briggs Amasco (Perfrisa), Cape (Unishield), H H Robertson (Trimawall and Trimaroof), and to panels with bonded insulation being available from British Steel (Warmclad), European Profiles and Ward Bros (Moduclad). It draws attention to the greater ease of installation of these systems over site-assembled insulation.

The ECCS has prepared recommendations for the design and installation of sandwich panels and the ECCS Working Party TWGT 7.4, which prepared this work, has extended it to cover a mineral wool core under the auspices of the CIB.*

A study for the Welsh Development Agency and the Building Research Energy Conservation Support Unit (BRECSU)[92] showed that composite panels can be installed more easily, more quickly and more effectively than site-assembled insulation, but drew no conclusions whether the technique was cost effective. The study referred to a policy WDA had already introduced — of conducting a thermographic survey on the completed building — to identify areas of misplaced insulation.

Agrément Certificates (or the local equivalent) have been issued for composite panels in Germany, France, Spain, Ireland and the UK, and the European Union of Agrément has prepared a Report on the assessment of composite panels with a CFC-free polyurethane foam core.[15]

Secret-fix systems
The standing seam is a traditional detail in lead work and work in other soft metals, but a standing-seam roof system in steel was introduced at the Chicago World Fair in 1934.[93] Butler Buildings reintroduced the system in America in 1969 and introduced it into Europe in 1973. The system uses roll-formed fluted panels whose edges are joined together on site by a mobile machine to form a sealed 360° double-lock seam.[94] Originally the system used aluminium alloy or aluminised steel, but aluminium–zinc alloy coated steel, stainless steel or coil-coated products have been introduced since 1973. (The lock seam involves more severe deformation than a conventional roll-formed profile, but the coating is able to accommodate this.) Kaiser Aluminium/Hoogovens offer an equivalent product, similar in

*CIB is the Conseil International du Bâtiment/International Council for Building Research Studies and Documentation — a separate organisation from the UK body which shares the same acronyn.

Table 20. Acceptance in standards of developments in design since 1976

Publication	Title	Date	Development covered
BS 5427: 1976	Performance and loading criteria for profiled sheet in building	1976	Reference to laminated panels (but no guidance on their use). Reference to curved panels (i.e. to preformed coated aluminium and asbestos cement). Reference to crown fixing for roofing to avoid leakage (i.e. no recognition of secret-fix systems).
PSA TB 509-200	Technical Guidance Sheet Cladding	1977	Includes detailed guidance on composite claddings in Section 2.4. Refers to availability of: traditional curved steel sheets with sinusoidal profile, curved sinusoidal and trapezoidal profiles in aluminium from Alcan and British Aluminium, curved trapezoidal profiles in steel from Ash & Lacy (Floclad) secret-fix systems (Cape Snaplap).
ECCS 20	The testing of profiled metal sheets	1978	No development covered, but states the recommendations (which are for steel construction) are also applicable for aluminium sheeting.
PSA MOB 01.705	Technical Guidance Sheet Cladding, Second Edition	1979	Little change from 1977 edition. Illustrates plank (Briggs – Amasco) and dished profiles (Gränges – Essem).
BRE Current paper CP6/79	Metal skinned sandwich panels for external walls	1979	Considers possible improvements in panel construction, control of manufacture, test methods for development and quality control.
Constrado	Profiled steel cladding and decking for commercial and industrial buildings	1980	Illustrates plank and ribbed profiles. Distinguishes between bonded insulated panels (e.g. Ward) and composite panels (H H Robertson). Illustrates Floclad curved sheets (Ash & Lacy) and Snaplap secret-fix system (Cape).
NFRC	Profiled sheet metal roofing and cladding — a guide to good practice	1982	Refers to curved sheets and composite panels. No reference to secret-fix systems.
ECCS 40	The design of profiled sheeting	1983	Covers ribbed profiles and curved trapezoidal profiles.
ECCS 41	Good practice in steel cladding and roofing	1983	Covers site-installed methods for insulation. Recognises composite panels exist, but not included in document.

Table 20. Continued

Publication	Title	Date	Development covered
PSA MOB 01 708	Technical Guidance Wall and Roof Cladding	1986	Gives separate guidance on site-installed sandwich insulation systems and composite panels. Discourages use of 'semi-composite systems' (bonded panels). Recognises standard reverse-side coating on steel is inadequate in corrosive conditions and that alternative specifications are available.
PSA MOB 01 709	Technical Guidance Roofing Systems (concealed fix low pitched)	1987	Gives detailed guidance on standing seam concealed fix systems for low pitched roofing (which have no fixing which penetrates the roof).
BRE Report	Thermal insulation: avoiding risks	1989	Covers use of composite panels: potential benefit in control of condensation, cautions against possibility of delamination.
ECCS 62	Preliminary European Recommendations for Sandwich Panels. Part II Good Practice	1990	Covers installation, inspection and maintenance of sandwich panels. Primarily considers rigid foam plastic core. Directed at manufacturer and specifier of product.
ECCS 66	Preliminary European Recommendations for Sandwich Panels. Part I Design	1991	Covers design and testing procedures for sandwich panels and their fastenings. Primarily considers rigid foam plastic core.
NFRC	Profiled sheet metal roofing and cladding — a guide to good practice	1991	Covers secret-fix systems, curved sheets and composite panels.
EPIC	Various	1991 to date	Cover use of composite panels.
MCRMA	Technical Papers 2, 3, 5, 6, 9 and 10	1991–5	Cover use of curved sheets, secret-fix systems, composite panels and mitred corners.
CIB* Report 148	Preliminary European Recommendations for Sandwich Panels with Additional Recommendations for panels with mineral wool core material	1991	Extends ECCS 66 to cover mineral wool core.
BRE Report	Thermal insulation: avoiding risks	1994	Repeats guidance in 1989 edition.
BS 5427: Part 1: 1996	The use of profiled sheet for roof and wall cladding on buildings	1996	Covers use of curved sheets, secret-fix systems and composite panels.

*See Clause 2.2.2 'Composite Panels'.

principle but differing in detail, in clad aluminium (aluminium faced with a different aluminium alloy) or coil-coated aluminium.[95]

Secret-fix systems can be installed from eaves to ridge, have sealed longitudinal joints, are fixed using fixing clips within the seam (i.e. fixings which do not penetrate the sheet) and hence can be used at a low pitch. (Typical pitches which are used to avoid ponding are for a design fall of 2.5° (1 in 23), which is expected to achieve a minimum finished fall of 1° (1 in 57).)

Some secret-fix systems can be installed to form a curved roof or a wave-formed curve. Secret fix details are also used to secure composite panels and it is possible to design the edge profile and overlap of a trapezoidally corrugated sheet so that the main fastening is concealed and overlapped by the adjacent sheet.

Roll forming on-site
Roll forming on-site is common in America and has been used in the UK to roll form gutters and downpipes from coated aluminium strip, and more rarely for cladding and roofing. Hoogovens and Plannja are now beginning to introduce the technique more widely as it enables large spans to be covered without joints and avoids the difficulties involved in transporting long roll-formed profiles.

2.2.3. Other developments in design

Curtain walling
There is already a substantial use of powder coatings on in-fill panels for curtain walling, but many of the other materials described in this chapter could also be produced in this form and used in curtain walling. These materials introduce no new requirements for installation or design and standard techniques can be used without modification.

Novel products produced by Alusingen for use in curtain walling are Alucobond Ecoclad, which uses sandwich panels of PVF_2-coated aluminium around a 3 mm polythylene core and holds an Avis Technique, and Alucore (a coil-coated aluminium facing over a honeycomb aluminium panel).[96]

Over the period considered there have been substantial improvements in the guidance available on curtain walling. BS 8200: 1985 *Code of Practice for design of non-loadbearing external vertical enclosures of buildings*[56] was published in 1985. The Centre for Window and Cladding Technology was set up at the University of Bath in 1989, produced their *Standard Guide to Good Practice for Curtain Walling* in 1993[6] and revised it in loose-leaf form in 1996.

Preformed metal tiles

There is a long history of use of pressed metal tiles as roofing in New Zealand, South Africa and Scandinavia. These tiles have been imported for some 20 years and some are now manufactured in the UK. The original specification was for a preformed galvanised steel tile, with a bitumen basecoat and coloured mineral chippings, and the tile was pressed from metal sheet in a form which simulated the appearance of several tiles which overlapped to give the appearance of a conventional tiled roof.

Scandinavian experience prefers the use of coil-coated sheet (polyester, plastisol or PVF_2), roll formed and pressed to shape, often simulating the appearance of more than one course of tiles, and in a variety of profiles which simulate different style tiles. Both galvanised steel and aluminium – zinc alloy coated steel are used as the base, but the only coil-coated tiles imported into the UK are those with a PVF_2 coating.

Other developments have been the use of sheet with a lower zinc coating weight (Z275) and an epoxy coil coating as a base for an acrylic basecoat and mineral chippings, the use of other coatings applied after forming, and the production of a slate profile. Heavier gauges of steel have been used for situations where abuse is possible and these products have been produced in lengths which enable them to be installed from eaves to ridge.

The proposed European Standards for self-supporting roofing in the pr EN 500 series[33,35] include requirements for dimensional tolerances for tiles (copper or zinc, pr EN 506 Annex A3; steel, pr EN 508-1 Annex B3; stainless steel, pr EN 508-3 Annex B3).

The market for preformed tiles is specialist, primarily in housing and particularly in refurbishment work (such as conversions from flat to pitched roofs) as they are light in weight and require little or no change to the existing structure. There is also an increasing market where the design is intended to simulate the appearance of housing, for example in sports buildings, or to reduce the visual impact of other buildings in or beside residential areas.

Bonded panels

Broderick Structures once produced chipboard panels with a facing of coil-coated aluminium, which overlapped at the edges. The aluminium alloy used was SIC/1200 in soft tempers. The panels were used for cladding or roofing and were jointed using traditional soft metal roofing techniques, with batten rolls or standing seams, in accordance with CP 143: Part 15: 1973.

As a result of changes in roof construction and insulation, Broderick Structures no longer produce roof panels in this form, but they continue to produce a bonded cladding panel, with a coil-coated facing on a particle board backing which is used on walls and mansard roofs. The edges of the panel are joined with standing seams or flattened seams and a factory-formed drip detail is used at horizontal lap joints.[97]

2.3. Trends in metals

BS 5427: 1976 covers the use of aluminium, galvanised steel and stainless steel profiles for roofing and cladding. It does not give a detailed specification for the physical properties or chemical composition of aluminium sheet, or for the properties, composition or coating weight of galvanised steel sheet, but refers instead to product standards and codes of practice for profiled sheet. (It gives no further guidance on stainless steel.)

2.3.1. Aluminium

BS 5427: 1976 makes reference to BS 4868: 1972 Specification for profiled aluminium sheet for building and CP 143: Part 1: 1958 Sheet roof and wall coverings: Part 1: Aluminium corrugated and troughed.

CP 143: Part 15: 1973 Sheet roof and wall coverings: Part 15: Aluminium covers aluminium installed by traditional roofing techniques (the techniques which are also used for other soft metals) and is relevant to this study although it is not covered by BS 5427: 1976.

In 1980, as part of an international agreement, British Standards adopted the use of the four-digit designation of the Aluminium Association for aluminium alloys, with the ISO chemical symbol designation in parallel, and discontinued the previous BS alloy designation. CEN has implemented the same agreement and aluminium alloys are now designated to the four-digit scale in EN 573-1, to the ISO chemical symbol scale in EN 573-2, and the composition limits are defined in EN 573-3. The composition requirements of the standards in use in 1976, converted to the current designations, and the requirements of current European draft standards for aluminium and roofing are compared in Table 21.

Like the 1976 edition, BS 5427: 1996 does not define the composition of aluminium alloys for roofing and cladding in detail, but refers to other standards — EN 485, BS 4868 and BS 8118. EN 485 gives general requirements for all aluminium alloys and does not consider the particular requirements of roofing and cladding. BS 4868: 1972 is still current, and continues to cover the two aluminium alloys 3103 and 3105. BS 8118: Part 1 gives a review of aluminium alloys suitable for use as building sheets in clause 2.2.1.1.3 and introduces a durability classification for alloys in Tables 2.2 and 2.6. The aluminium alloys available in sheet with the highest (A) classification for durability are included in Table 21.

The *Fulmer Materials Optimiser*[98] also gives a useful summary of the properties of aluminium alloys. The properties considered most relevant for this application are tensile strength, resistance to atmospheric attack and suitability for cold forming — these ratings are also included in Table 21.

2.3.2. Galvanised steel

BS 5427: 1976 makes reference to BS 3083: 1959 Hot-dipped galvanised corrugated steel sheets for general purposes and CP 143: Part 10: 1973 Sheet roof and wall coverings: galvanised corrugated steel.

These standards cover the use of galvanised steel with no organic coating and their requirements for zinc coating weight are based on the life this alone achieves. The standards give no guidance on the zinc coating weight that is appropriate for the base of a coated steel sheet. BS 5427 gives the life to first maintenance for metal finishes on steel in Table D2 but does not define the appropriate zinc thickness for use with an organic coating in Tables E1 and E3.

The use of coated steel sheet was also recognised in Schedule 5 to Regulation A16 of the Building Regulations 1976*[99] which accepted

(*a*) galvanised sheet steel complying with class 1A of BS 2989: 1975 or type 200 of BS 3083: 1959

or

(*b*) sheet steel which is vitreous enamelled or coated with bitumen or other organic substance of like durability during the course of manufacture

as suitable for the external surface of the walls and roofs of permanent buildings. Schedule 9 (to Regulation E1)* recognised the use of 'PVC-coated steel' as a covering for pitched roofs. The changes that have taken place in these documents and their requirements for galvanised steel are described in Table 22.

Requirements for galvanised steel in current specifications and drafts are included in the following standards.

*Comparable text was included in the Regulations for Scotland and Northern Ireland.

(a) BS 6781:1986   EU 169 — 1985 Continuously organic coated steel flat products

This standard had no definitive requirements for zinc coating weight, but anticipated that a Z275 (or thicker) coating will be used.

(b) EN 10169-1996   Continuously organic coated (coil-coated) steel flat products — Part 1 General information

This standard, which has been issued in the BS EN series (to replace BS 6781) allows the application of organic coatings to steel with no metal coating (for other uses, not for building) and otherwise expects galvanised steel to EN 10142 or 10147 to be used.

(c) pr EN 10169-2   Continuously organic coated steel flat products — products for building exterior applications

This requires the basic strip to satisfy EN 10142 or 10147 with a minimum coating weight in accordance with the appropriate national regulations for the country of use.

(d) pr EN 505   Roofing products from metal sheet — specification for fully supported products of steel sheet

(e) pr EN 508-1   Roofing products from metal sheet — specification for self-supporting products of steel sheet — steel

Both roofing standards describe the use of Z200, 225 or 275 sheet with an organic coating, and Z275, 350 and 450 uncoated. In Annex C they describe the UK requirements as Z275 with an organic coating and Z350 uncoated.

Key to Table 21

*The *Fulmer Materials Optimiser* uses the scales described below and gives the following ratings (for zero temper material).

Rating	Tensile strength MPa	Qualitative rating for atmospheric attack and cold forming
0	—	Unsuitable
1	14–70	Poor
2	71–140	Fair
3	141–210	Good
4	211–280	Very good
5	281–350	Excellent
6	>351	

†The alloys listed in CP 143: Part 1 as suitable for flashings are also listed in BS 5427: 1976, for the same purpose.

‡pr EN 507 and 508-2 require these alloys to be coated and do not allow them in an uncoated condition.

Table 21. Summary of requirements for aluminium alloys in previous and current standards and drafts

Four-digit designation EN 573-1	ISO designation EN 573-2	Previous BS designation	BS 4846	Sheet	Flashings†	CP 143 Pt 15	EN 1396	pr EN 507	pr EN 508-2	BS 8118 Pt 1	Tensile strength	Atmospheric attack	Cold forming
				CP 143 Pt 15			Requirements in current drafts & standards				Fulmer Materials Optimiser*		
1199	Al 99.99	S1			√	√					1	5	5
1080A	Al 99.8	S1A			√	√					2	5	5
1050A	Al 99.5	S1B				√	√	√			2	4	5
1200	Al 99.0	S1C			√	√	√	√‡		√	2	4	5
3003	Al Mn1Cu						√	√	√				
3004	Al Mg1						√	√	√				
3005	Al Mn1Mg0.5						√	√	√				
3103	AlMn1	NS3		√		√	√	√	√	√	2	4	5
3105	AlMnMg	NS31	√				√	√	√	√	2	4	4
5005	AlMg1						√		√‡		2	4	4
5050	Al Mg1.5						√						
5052	Al Mg2.5						√		√				
5083	Al Mg4.5 Mn0.7									√	5	4	3
5154A	Al Mg3.5									√	4	4	4
5182	Al Mg4.5 Mn0.4						√						
5251	Al Mg2	NS4			√		√		√	√	3	4	4
5454	Al Mg3Mn						√			√	4	4	4
5754	Al Mg3						√						
6011	Al NMg0.9 Si0.9Cu						√						
8011A	AlFeSi						√	√‡	√‡				

Table 22. Summary of requirements and designations for galvanised steel in previous and current standards

Previous standard	Requirements/comments			Current standard	Requirements/comments		
BS 5427: 1976 Table D2	Predicted life to first maintenance for galvanised steel (with no organic coating) (years)			**BS 5427: 1996** Table C2	Functional life of profiled materials (years)		
C (275) H1 (350)	Coastal	Ind/urban	Sub/rural		Coastal	Ind/urban	Sub/rural
H2 (450) H3 (600)	2–5 2–5 5–10 10–20	2–5 2–5 2–5 5–10	5–10 5–10 10–20 20–50	350	2–5	2–5	5–10
E1, E3	No requirement for zinc coating thickness when organic coating is present			D2, D4	Unchanged		
	Cross reference to CP 143: Part 10 and BS 3083				Reference to BS 3083 retained New ref. to BS 5950: Parts 6, 7 and 9 CP 143: Part 10 obsolescent.		
BS 3083: 1959	Type 200 (600 g m^{-2}) for use 'where conditions demand highest class coating weight'			**BS 3083: 1988**	Coatings retained, now designated G600		
	Type 150 (450 g m^{-2}) for 'use where conditions demand medium class coating weight'				G450		
	Type 120 (350 g m^{-2}) for 'use where conditions warrant a light class coating weight'				G350		
					Standard now also covers aluminium–zinc coated steel Requirements for steel to have minimum yield strength of 210 MPa, or for structural grade to be used if appropriate		
CP 143 Part 10 1973	No separate requirements on composition or coating weight — cross reference to BS 3083				Standard to be incorporated into BS 5427: Part 2		
BS 2989: 1975	Coating weights represented by previous designations: C 275 g m^{-2} H1 350 g m^{-2} H2 450 g m^{-2} H3 600 g m^{-2}			**EN 10142 10143 10147**	Separate standards for non-structural and structural grades Current designations: Z 275 Z 350 Z 450 Z 600		
Building Regulations 1976	Schedule 5 Tables 1 & 2 (to Reg A16)			**Building Regulations 1991**	Fundamental change in criteria for 'short-lived materials'		
	Schedule 9 Part 11 (to Reg E1)				Wider criteria for materials in Approved Document B Table A5 Parts ii and v		

(f) BS 5950: Part 7   Structural use of steelwork in building — specification for materials and workmanship: cold-formed sections
This standard refers to BS 2989 and EN 10142 and anticipates that the former will be replaced by subsequent European work. It allows other specifications to be used at the designers' discretion.

All these standards also allow the use of other metal coatings on steel which are considered in the following section.

2.3.3. Other metal coatings on steel

Besides its references to galvanised steel, BS 5427: 1976 also makes reference to aluminised steel type 2, which was in use in the UK in 1976. It predicted a long life (10–20 years) in coastal, industrial and urban surroundings and a very long life (20–50 years) in suburban and rural surroundings. These predictions were for the product without an organic coating and the standard did not anticipate that an organic coating would be applied.

Aluminised steel (type 2) was awarded Agrément Certificate 77/489, which was renewed as 82/939. The latter Certificate also described the possibility of coil coating the product. Agrément Certificate 78/526, an early Certificate for a secret-fix system, also included aluminised steel as one of the options available.

Aluminised steel (type 1) with an aluminium–silicon (5–11%) alloy coating was previously covered by BS 6536, ISO 5000 and Euronorm 154. These have now been replaced by EN 10154, which imposes a tighter requirement for silicon of 8–11%.

British Steel have considered producing aluminised steel but have chosen not to do so for commercial reasons. The commercial use of aluminised steel in the UK for building applications has always been small, and its use was seriously affected when British Steel began to produce the aluminium–zinc coated steel Zalutite. However, BS 6781, pr EN 10169-2, pr EN 505 and pr EN 508-1 all accept the use of aluminised steel. The two roofing drafts describe a UK requirement of $230\,\mathrm{g\,m^{-2}}$ (including both sides) for the aluminium coating, but describe the use of aluminised steel with an organic coating as 'not permitted by UK regulations'. Reference to aluminised steel is not included in BS 5427: 1996.

Although aluminium and zinc have much the same chemical reactivity, their protective effect on steel is substantially different. Aluminium metal is relatively inert, despite its reactive character, as the metal forms a coherent oxide film which protects the underlying metal from further oxidation. In the same way the surface of aluminised steel also has this coherent surface of aluminium oxide.

Zinc oxide does not have the same character with the result that a zinc surface is not protected in the same way, but becomes eroded at a uniform rate. At a damaged area or at the edge of a galvanised steel sheet, the effect is that an electrolytic cell is formed — the more reactive zinc dissolves in a sacrificial manner and protects the underlying steel from corrosion.

The coherent film of aluminium oxide prevents an effective electrolytic cell being formed with aluminised steel, with the result that the aluminium tends not to dissolve and the damaged area or edge of the sheet becomes rusted. This effect is self-limiting, as the coherent aluminium oxide layer tends to merge with the rusted area and so prevent further attack, and the overall effect is to extend the protective life substantially (over what would be expected from galvanised steel) but to prejudice its appearance in the short term.

The desirability of a compromise product, offering galvanic protection to cut edges and the durability associated with aluminium coating is obvious. Bethlehem Steel developed such a product, an aluminium – zinc (55:45) alloy coated steel, and began to produce it under the name Galvalume in 1972. Swedish Steel have produced it under licence (as Aluzinc) since 1980 and British Steel have done so (as Zalutite) since 1986. Before 1986 there was some British experience with imported material and one of the options offered by Butler Buildings with their secret-fix system was aluminium – zinc coated steel. There has also been substantial Australian experience and an early British application (for the uncoated product) was for the canopies of petrol stations. A recent development to improve the long-term appearance of uncoated aluminium – zinc alloy coated steel is the introduction of Acrylume, a clear polymer-coated form of Galvalume produced by US Steel.

The uncoated product was previously covered by BS 6830: 1987 and is now covered by EN 10215: 1995, is included in BS 3083: 1988, and is the subject of Agrément Certificates 87/1869 and 93/2971. BS 5427: 1996 includes aluminium – zinc coated steel and predicts a life (for the $185\,\mathrm{g\,m^{-2}}$ product without organic coating) of 10–20 years in coastal surroundings and more than 20 years in industrial, urban, suburban and rural surroundings.

BS 6781/Euronorm 169 was issued before any standard was prepared for aluminium – zinc alloy coated steel and so does not mention the product. EN 10169-1 (the current reissue of this standard) and pr EN 10169-2 for coated steel, and pr EN 505 and pr EN 508-1 for steel roofing all accept the use of the product. The two roofing drafts define UK requirements as being $185\,\mathrm{g\,m^{-2}}$ for the product without an organic

Table 23. Summary of bend test requirements for galvanised steel, zinc – aluminium (ZA) and aluminium – zinc (AZ) alloys

EN Standard	Coating	Coating weight (g m^{-2})	Coating thickness (µm)	Bend test requirements*
Forming grades 10142	Zinc	275 350	19.5 24.8	0 1a
10214	ZA	255 300	21.6 25.4	0 1a
10215	AZ	150 185	19.9 24.6	0 0 or 1a†
Structural grades 10147	Zinc	275 350	19.5 24.8	1a to 3a† 1a to 3a†
10214	ZA	255 300	21.6 25.4	0 to 1a‡ 1a to 2a‡
10215	AZ	150 185	19.9 24.6	1a to 3a† 1a to 3a†

*The bent test requirement relates the **diameter** of the mandrel to the thickness of the sheet, so that a requirement of 1a requires the mandrel's diameter to be the thickness of the sheet. (Note that standards for **organic** coatings on metals require the mandrel's **radius** to be related to the thickness of the sheet.)

†Requirement depends on the grade of steel.

‡Requirements quoted are for sheet up to 1.5 mm thick. The requirements for thicker sheets are 1a to 2a and 2a to 3a. Other standards do not differentiate between sheet thicknesses.

coating, and 150 g m^{-2} for the coil-coated product. British Steel (PVF$_2$, polyester, silicone – polyester), Dobel (PVF$_2$, plastisol, polyester) and Cockerill Sambre (PVF$_2$, plastisol) all supply the 150 g m^{-2} product, coil coated.

Development has also taken place with zinc – aluminium alloys with a lower proportion of aluminium. The International Lead Zinc Research Organisation has developed a 95:5 alloy, Galfan, and many European steel producers hold a licence and both produce and coil coat Galfan-coated steel. The product is covered by EN 10214, and EN 10169-1, pr EN 10169-2, pr EN 505 and pr EN 508-1 all accept its use. The roofing drafts define the UK requirements as being for the base sheet to have a metal coating weight of 255 g m,$^{-2}$ and to be coil coated.

The corrosion characteristics are substantially similar to those of galvanised steel, but such alloys are able to meet more exacting bend test requirements than galvanised steel or aluminium – zinc coated steel. The bend test requirements for galvanised steel, zinc – aluminium (ZA) coated steel, and aluminium–zinc (AZ) coated steel, taken from EN 10142, 10147, 10214 and 10215 are summarised in Table 23.

There is some Japanese experience with a 99:1 zinc:aluminium coated steel and this product is available in Europe. The benefits, if any, from this product are not known.

Much of the background knowledge on Zn:Al coated steels is on external exposure of the uncoated products, with the result that there has been little systematic study on the coatings' protective effect on cut edges, particularly when an organic coating is also present. The University of Manchester Institute of Science and Technology (UMIST) Corrosion and Protection Centre are conducting an investigation funded by the Engineering and Physical Sciences Research Council (EPSRC): Materials for Better Construction Initiative. The study includes electrochemical tests and measurements of paint undercutting on coil-coated Zn:Al coated steels (95:5 and 45:55) and on coil-coated galvanised steel, and is capable of investigating the different effects of chromium-based and chromium-free primers and pretreatments. Related work is being conducted at the Faculty of Engineering and Applied Science at Aston University (which includes studies on different materials in contact with the coated steels) and at the University of Wales, Swansea (where British Steel is an active partner).

The effect of aluminium in the alloy coating is to change the character of the surface of any exposed steel, i.e. for aluminium oxide to be present in the surface. If a chromate-based primer or pretreatment is used chromium oxides will be present on the exposed steel surface, and the active ingredient from any chrome-free alternative will perform in the same way. It is considered that surface analytical techniques could be able to determine the nature and extent of the chemical changes taking place on the surface, and it is recommended that surface techniques such as scanning electron microscopy (SEM), inductively coupled mass spectrometry (ICMS), or energy dispersive X-ray scattering (EDXS) should be considered for this purpose.

2.3.4. Stainless steel

BS 5427: 1976 refers to the use of profiles of stainless steel or of stainless steel clad mild steel, and to the possibility of obtaining a durable colour finish by using a chemical treatment. The current revision of the standard refers only to profiled stainless steel and does not mention stainless steel clad mild steel or chemical treatment, but colour finishes by this process are still available.

pr EN 502 and 508-3 both refer to ferritic, austenitic and austenitic-molybdenum stainless steels and allow them to be used uncoated, with a metal coating (of tin or terne) and/or with an organic coil coating. The coil coatings described are polyester, silicone–polyester, polyurethane, PVF$_2$ and plastisol. There is little experience of organic-coated stainless steel in the UK. British Steel are able to produce PVF_2-coated austenitic stainless steel (Hyclad),[100] but this product is expected to be for export markets rather than for use in the UK.

2.3.5. Other metals

Both editions of BS 5427 cover the use of steel or aluminium, but neither anticipate the use of other metals. The Secretary of State's Guidance Notes[79] describe coil coating of steel, stainless steel, aluminium or copper, EN 501 indicates that zinc can be coil coated 'for special architectural reasons' (not as routine), and pr EN 506 describes coil coatings for copper or zinc (acrylic, polyester, silicone – polyester, PVF_2 or plastisol) or the use of a pre-weathered surface.[33]

Colour-coated lead is available from Calder Industrial Materials, but is produced in widths more appropriate for flashings rather than cladding or roofing.

There is some Japanese experience of coil-coated copper, but the only experience in the UK and elsewhere in Europe of the coated materials described in this section are for pre-weathered copper. It is considered that there is little advantage in coil coating metals which already have a satisfactory performance and attractive appearance in the uncoated condition, and it is expected that commercial use of coil-coated zinc, lead and copper will be small.

2.4. Conclusions

The review of developments considered in this chapter was conducted with reference to 1976, when the use of coated metal roofing and cladding had become relatively well established.

2.4.1. Coatings

In 1976 the coatings in use were predominantly plastisol on steel, PVF_2 on aluminium, and polyester, applied by coil coating. Since 1976 there has been substantial development of plastisol and polyester, and multicoat PVF_2 systems have been introduced.

New coil coatings introduced since 1976 have been abrasion-resistant systems on aluminium and multicoat polyurethane systems on steel. Polyester powder coatings (applied in a conventional powder coating plant) have come into widespread use on cladding panels. Other developments in powder coatings are the use of PVF_2 powder coating, and the application of powder coatings in a powder coil-coating line, but these developments have yet to be fully exploited.

The use of laminates (where a plastic film is applied in a coil-coating line) is low.

The UK is committed to reduce national emissions of VOCs by 30% between 1988 and 1999. The use of coil coatings (with the exhaust gases incinerated — the routine procedure used by the industry) or of powder coatings enables painted products to be produced without emission of VOCs.

The case for the replacement of chromium in pretreatments and primers was examined. It was concluded that the technical advantages associated with the use of chromium were high, that the technical risks from using relatively unproven alternative materials for long-term external uses were not justified, and that the risks from using chrome-based products in properly controlled automated plants were low. The environmental case against PVC was also considered and it was concluded that there is no realistic technical or environmental case against PVC or plasticised PVC under current conditions of manufacture and use.

A range of coatings and coating systems exist for application to cut edges of steel sheet or for the repair of corroded installations. The use of these materials can be laborious and it is recommended that measures should be taken in the design to minimise the extent of exposed cut edges in order to reduce the need for these products to be used.

2.4.2. Design

Developments in design since 1976 have included the use of curved sheet, laminated and composite panels, standing-seam and concealed-fix systems, tapered curves, and the widespread use of preformed metal tiles. These developments have extended the range of design options available to the user of coil-coated metals (and give some of the flexibility in design which has always been available with powder-coating). These developments involve more severe forming conditions than the routine trapezoidal profile — it is recognised that the commercial success and widespread use of these developments demonstrate that the metals and coatings used are able to accommodate these severe forming conditions on a routine production basis.

2.4.3. Metals

Since 1976 a wider range of aluminium alloys has become available for coil coating and for use in roofing and cladding.

There have been changes in galvanised steel in respect of its designation and base steels used, but there have been no technical changes in respect of coating weight or its ability to accept paint.

There have been substantial changes in the metal coatings used on steel and zinc–aluminium coated steels (Zn:Al 99:1, 95:5 and 45:55) are now available (and aluminised steel continues to be available). These alloy coatings may confer corrosion protection on steel by a different mechanism to a galvanised coating, and are the subject of three studies conducted in the EPSRC Materials for Better Construction Initiative. It is considered that surface analytical techniques could be used to study the chemical changes taking place on the surface (which arise both from these alloy coatings and from corrosion-inhibiting primers and pretreatments) and it is recommended that such work should be included in existing programmes, or commissioned separately.

Coil-coated stainless steel is available and is a potentially long-life material.

Other metals can be coil coated, but no benefit or commercial advantage can be identified from doing so.

2.5. Recommendations

Many of the developments described in this chapter are included in the 1996 edition of BS 5427, in new European standards for general uses of coil-coated metal, or are covered by current European work which has not yet been completed. These standards are considered in more detail and recommendations concerning them are given in Chapter 4.

Other recommendations are that:

(a) Specifiers, clients and designers should use measures in design and installation which reduce the extent of exposed cut edges on steel cladding and roofing

(b) Support for existing research on the performance of steel cladding and roofing should continue, and the research should be extended to include:

  (i) an investigation of the influence of different alloy coatings and different thicknesses of alloy coatings, chrome-based and chrome-free primers and pretreatments, different reverse-side coating specifications, and different cutting techniques on the performance of exposed cut edges of coil-coated steel cladding and roofing

  (ii) an exposure programme to investigate the influence of different alloy coatings and coating thicknesses on the overall durability of coil-coated steel cladding and roofing (this programme could be extended to investigate the durability of the alloy-coated steel with no coil coating)

(iii) an investigation of the influence of different alloy coatings and different primers and pretreatments on the character of the surface of exposed steel, by surface analytical techniques

(c) Due recognition should be given to the contribution that precoated metal roofing and cladding (which are coated in controlled conditions in industrial processes such as coil coating and powder coating) can make to meeting national commitments on emissions of volatile organic compounds.

3. International comparison

This chapter examines the use of organically coated metals as roofing and cladding outside the UK through a combination of correspondence and meetings with approval bodies, trade associations, manufacturers and specifiers. Visits carried out to existing sites in Europe and the United States are detailed and the general situation of the industry in Europe, the United States and Australasia is discussed.

3.1. Europe (excluding the United Kingdom)

3.1.1. Trade associations and other organisations

Questionnaires were sent to a total of 18 European organisations thought to be active in this product area. The questionnaire asked for details of the materials commonly used, anticipated and achieved lifetimes and problems encountered in service. Four replies were received from Austria, and single replies came from organisations in Ireland, Norway and Germany. Summaries of these surveys can be found in Appendix 2 of this report.

The materials used vary between countries and also (in the case of Austria) depending on the area of expertise of the organisation but, with the exception of Ireland, all were manufactured in the country in question. The stated life expectancy was found to range from 15 years for plastisol-coated galvanised steel in Ireland to a claimed 100 years for coil- and powder-coated products in Austria, although most replies anticipate a 20–30 year lifetime. Four respondents had experienced no problems in service; corrosion was reported at edges in one case and at chipped areas in another, and one contact described chalking of polyester powder coatings.

In the United Kingdom, construction products not adequately covered by Standards may be awarded a Certificate on the basis of their fitness for purpose by the British Board of Agrément as described in Section 1.1.1 of this report. Other European nations operate their own Agrément approval bodies in the same way. It is possible for an Agrément Certificate awarded in one country to be published (after an assessment of the data on which it is based) in a second country by the national Agrément body by a process known as Confirmation. However the BBA has no knowledge of any current Confirmations relating to organically coated metal roofing or cladding.

The Swiss-based Qualicoat approval system sets out requirements for paint, lacquer and powder coatings on aluminium for architectural purposes. It is particularly recognised in France, Spain, Italy, Benelux countries and Greece. An approval can be issued only to a coating plant and is awarded after the satisfactory completion of a comprehensive testing schedule on the coated product to ensure compliance with the Qualicoat specifications and two inspections of the coater's equipment, production process, laboratory facilities and quality control documentation. Following approval, routine inspections are made between two and five times per year to ensure that the standards are being maintained. Repeat testing is also carried out on an annual basis.

The GSB approved system is a similar process based in Germany and more commonly used in that country and Scandinavia. It publishes technical guidelines for the piecework coating of building materials and so, like Qualicoat, is more relevant for powder than coil coating. It also requires pre-approval testing and inspection and an annual confirmation process.

From Spring 1997, companies wishing to export steel products of the type under consideration into Germany must apply to the German Authorities for Ü Mark Approval. This requires compliance with the relevant German DIN standards and subsequent inspection and repeat testing to ensure that this performance is being maintained. This is said to be a temporary process until the procedures are in place to allow the use of CE marking for the products. The UK Government has objected to this procedure as being against the provisions of Article 16 of the Construction Products Directive. A guidance paper has been drafted by the Department of the Environment and the National Council of Building Materials Producers, in conjunction with the German Standards body DIBt, on the requirements of the Ü Mark legislation for UK manufacturers.

The European Coil Coating Association (ECCA) serves not only the construction industry, but also other product areas likely to use coil-coated materials, such as the automotive and electrical industries. They have estimated that since the 1960s over eight billion square metres of pre-coated material have been produced: approximately 48.7 million square metres of steel and 15.6 million square metres of aluminium were coated for the European construction industry in 1995. Of this, it was estimated that approximately 55% of coatings were polyester, 30% plastisol and 5% PVF_2, with the balance being made up by more specialist small-volume coatings.

In addition to their primary activity of promotion of the coil-coating industry, the ECCA operate four natural weathering sites, in Holland (one in a marine/industrial environment and one in an inland industrial), Portugal (high UV) and France (marine).[8] The first three were visited as part of this work. Samples are exposed both as control/development projects for client companies and by the ECCA itself to document the corrosivity of the sites. The samples are arranged at three inclinations — 45° South, 5° South and 90° North — and detailed records are maintained of the climatic conditions. A very wide range of products is exposed on these sites, and while for reasons of client confidentiality it was not possible to discuss individual samples, examples were noted of cut edge corrosion in certain cases after only two years exposure.

The limited information available indicated that the materials used and experience of the products available varies widely within individual nations. Three countries known to have a tradition of use of these materials are therefore examined in more detail below.

3.1.2. Holland

Independent consultant/research agency
A visit was made to the offices of an independent consultant and research agency specialising in a number of fields, including construction. The individuals concerned had up to 25 years experience of the country's cladding and roofing industry, including inspections of sites where problems had been encountered (on average one or two per month).

It was said that galvanised steel was the most commonly used substrate in Holland, with approximately 20% using aluminium and a small amount of aluminium–zinc alloy coated steel. The latter has a reputation for suffering from coating problems in Holland. The most common problems found on-site were said to be cracking of galvanising where the product was roll formed. This often occurs even on relatively light bends.

Early PVF_2 materials were said to have suffered from delamination but this was no longer felt to be a significant problem with modern formulations.

Coatings are normally covered by a ten-year warranty in Holland provided by the cladding supplier although certain companies have begun to offer a 15-year guarantee. This covers coating integrity and colour change (including chalking). Overcoating is common in the case of failure although experience has shown that this is difficult for older coatings which are thought to embrittle on ageing.

The company visited is active in materials research, operates its own exposure site and also uses commercial facilities elsewhere in Holland. Examination of samples on-site showed examples of edge corrosion and delamination particularly with plastisol, and of corrosion at folded edges. A report on this work is due to be published by the consultants in 1997.

A previously published Dutch paper[101] describes work carried out on a selection of 13 commercially available coil-coated metal products together with three reference materials used in the same areas but applied by different techniques. The aim was to determine their performance in mechanical testing and natural and artificial weathering.

The products involved a combination of substrates (aluminium, galvanised steel and aluminium–zinc alloy coated steel), pretreatment, primers and top-coats (including polyesters, polyurethanes, PVF_2 and plastisol) chosen to show the effect of changing these variables. A wide variety of relevant tests were carried out to ascertain all aspects of the products' performance.

A problem was noted with the mechanical testing carried out in that the standard test methods used did not always accurately measure the intended property. In these tests the substrate and pretreatment/primer chosen was found to have a significant effect on the systems' performance with the galvanised samples but had only a small influence on the aluminium samples. Overall the aluminium substrates gave the best flexibility, followed by the galvanised steel, with the aluminium–zinc alloy coated steel being the least flexible. Only the plastisol sample showed any signs of cracking of the galvanising at the formed edge — these samples could be formed to a more acute angle due to the known flexibility of the coating system. Adhesion was very good in all cases with other properties such as impact resistance and pencil hardness varying between the systems tested.

Both artificial weathering (1000 hours to ISO/DIS 11341/DIN 53231/ ECCA T/10) and natural exposure were included in the test programme. For the natural exposure, results were discussed after two years exposure at three different Dutch sites and after 18 months in Florida. Panels were exposed at 45° South, 5° South and 90° North. Two aspects of performance were considered following these exposures — weathering and corrosion resistance.

The assessment of weathering was found to be difficult since there exists a lack of recognised test methods for the rating of performance and of weighting the various properties measured. The coil-coated samples were generally assessed as performing well and (with the exception of one polyester system on galvanised steel) were rated as superior to the reference systems. The weathering resistance is primarily a function of the top-coat: in general terms the PVF_2 systems were rated above the polyester/polyamides which were themselves superior to the polyesters and plastisol. It was decided not to rank the individual systems, however, since the time of exposure was too short in relation to the anticipated life expectancy of the products.

Variations were found to exist on the performance of the products based on the site chosen and the orientation of the samples. A Dutch coastal site produced weathering approximately one and a half times more severe than a more inland site; Florida exposure showed no more severe weathering than that in Holland (and chalking was produced more rapidly in Holland). Weathering of 45° South panels produced results about twice as severe as those weathered at 90° North.

The correlation between natural and artificial weathering was assessed as being very poor, both for colour retention and, particularly, gloss retention. It was estimated that 1000 hours artificial weathering under the given conditions approximated to two years at 45° South in coastal Holland.

In addition to the weathering tests, other accelerated corrosion tests were investigated including neutral and (for aluminium only) acetic acid salt fog tests. A single figure corrosion index system was proposed for the assessment of panels after testing. Performance in natural and accelerated artificial corrosion testing was found to be influenced by substrate, pretreatment and top-coat. Of the top-coat tests, PVF_2 was again rated superior to polyester/polyamide with polyesters ranking last.

In natural weathering, aluminium was the best performing substrate for corrosion resistance. Aluminium – zinc alloy coated steel was found to be inferior to galvanised steel after two years exposure, although earlier Japanese work[102] has shown that these relative performances are reversed after nine years exposure (exposure is continuing to determine whether this process is reproduced).

The correlation between natural exposure and artificial acceleration of corrosion was found to be poor, particularly for the salt fog testing, and to depend upon the materials chosen, orientation of panels, etc. The morphology of the resulting corrosion products was found to vary depending on the test method chosen. It was concluded that specifications for coated metals should include a requirement for natural exposure in addition to accelerated testing. Some work is known to have been carried out in an attempt to devise a more realistic and reproducible artificial weathering test, usually involving a more complex group of electrolytes and cyclic conditions. An example of this is the Prohesion test, which is described in Annex D to pr EN 10169-2 and is increasingly used by the UK industry. The company visited has been active in this area of research and has developed a test that can be used for both galvanised and aluminium substrates, involving a 24 h cycle of changing temperatures and humidities and the use of a fog of artificial rainwater containing a controlled level of electrolytes, carbon dioxide and sulphur dioxide. This test cycle is claimed to produce realistic corrosion pattern and to provide results that closely match those found in actual service.

From the results of the work reported here, the authors predicted life expectancies of some of the products based on their performance in weathering and corrosion tests. The difficulties in assigning such figures from the available data was acknowledged, both in terms of the quantity of data available and the differing visual standards applied to completed buildings in varying service conditions. However, for middle to high ranking aesthetic requirements, one polyester system had a predicted life expectancy of only five years and the reference samples of 5–10 years. The other products were superior but no figures were given. For the better performing products corrosion resistance is more significant. The life expectancy of 'good' systems was said to be more than ten years with more than 30 years attainable for several of the tested systems.

Trade association
A visit was made to a trade organisation set up to represent the interests of the Dutch metal industry.

It was estimated by this organisation that the use of cladding accounts for between 10% and 20% of the Dutch construction industry, amounting to an annual expenditure of around £300 million.

The major area of current concern was said to be the lack of available training for the labour force. There exists a core of highly experienced and competent individuals at a supervisory level, but the majority of the actual installers are employed on a short-term basis for specific projects and so fall outside of company training schemes. This often results in poor site workmanship and premature failures of the cladding. (Failures caused by faults inherent to the materials themselves are said to be rare and are rectified under the warranties already referred to.)

In consultation with major manufacturers, an attempt is being made in Holland to introduce an education programme, ideally with some form of compulsion, for completion by all site employees. It is intended that such a course will concentrate on health and safety issues as this has been the cause of some concern within the industry and it is not yet clear how much emphasis will be placed on the improvement of installation standards.

Coil coater
A further visit was made to a coil-coater/system manufacturer. This company group manufactures the coatings used and applies them

exclusively to aluminium (unspecified problems having been encountered in the past with steel substrates) for the construction of composite cladding panels. There is little or no market for this product as a roofing material. (In general in Holland commercial roofs are commonly flat and domestic roofs are constructed of concrete tiles although organically coated metal roofs are also encountered.) Toll coaters are also used where the necessary coils cannot be processed in-house.

The aluminium substrates are supplied to an agreed EN-based specification. Quality problems have been encountered in the past and all suppliers must now be ISO 9001 registered. Coating specifications are written around the performance criteria of EN 1396 Annex C and no testing is carried out, reliance being placed on this specification.

It was said that most panels in Holland are roll formed to give male and female panel edges. These are interlocked when installed to prevent cut edges from being exposed. Secret fixing is the recommended practice in all cases, although this manufacturer tends to supply only to the high specification projects and it is recognised that this form of fixing is very unlikely to be used in basic industrial units.

The most commonly encountered failure was reported to be substrate corrosion although this had been greatly reduced by changing the supply regime. Coating problems are extremely rare even though buildings are often poorly designed and subject to little or no routine maintenance (the manufacturer recommends annual washing but this is rarely performed).

The company offers a ten-year warranty on their products. This guarantees the integrity of the film, an even colour with a maximum colour change, ΔE of two over this period and chalking of less than two on the ECCA scale.

Site inspection
A number of site inspections were also carried out to investigate the actual performance of Dutch cladding and roofing. This was only practicable with the cooperation of local manufacturers, who were able to suggest suitable sites and accompany the BBA inspector during the visit to help with access. This meant that the BBA were not involved in site selection and may have meant that only high-quality high-performing buildings were viewed. However, the opportunity was also taken to examine any other suitable buildings in the vicinity, even though no information would be available on age, materials or construction. As a result, no attempt has been made to carry out a full statistical analysis of these results. They should be taken only as an indication of the types of problems commonly found in Dutch

construction. (These comments apply equally to sites visited in other countries and summarised elsewhere in this report.)

The involvement of the manufacturers meant that full details were usually provided for the main sites. In some cases access was limited and it was not possible to obtain full data on the construction used (e.g. composite panels or built up construction). Brief summaries of the sites seen are given in Table 24.

Chapter 4 of this report describes the current European Standards that have been published by the BSI on organically coated metals for use as cladding and roofing and discusses the way in which these documents have replaced earlier British Standards where necessary.

Table 24. Sites in Holland

Site ref.	Area	Construction	Materials	Comments
H1	Industrial building near motorway in Rotterdam — age not known	Composite panel cladding with secret fixing	Polyurethane-coated aluminium	Edges had been incorrectly cut leading to a coarse rough finish. This had been overcoated with a remedial coating which was showing signs of failure. Otherwise in excellent condition.
H2	Industrial building in Rotterdam — six years old	Composite panel cladding with secret fixing	Polyurethane-coated aluminium	Very good condition throughout
H3	Leisure building in coastal Rotterdam — two years old	Composite panel cladding with secret fixing	PVF_2-coated aluminium	Some dirt retention caused by the building design and detailing, the nature of the location and lack of maintenance. Otherwise very good condition.
H4	Leisure building in rural location near a small lake — seven years old	Single-skin roofing with standing seam	PVF_2-coated aluminium	Some sheet overlaps had been welded and overcoated. Although not readily visible, this had caused colour variation.
H5	Leisure building in an urban area — seventeen years old	Single-skin roofing with standing seam	PVF_2-coated aluminium	A copper lightning conductor had been installed without the necessary insulation, leading to bimetallic corrosion. Other problems included minor edge corrosion and staining caused by poor detailing.
H6	Leisure building in urban Amsterdam — between one and five years old	Cladding and roofing	Believed to be aluminium substrate. Powder coated in-fill panels and polyester coil-coated roof	Generally excellent condition. One case of poor workmanship with fixings.

A similar situation exists in other European countries whereby existing national standards are being supplemented and/or superseded by these European Standards. The number and scope of standards involved varies country by country and it is not practicable to compile a comprehensive list: however, the situation existing in the European countries under investigation has been examined to provide a comparison with the UK position.

Holland has no national standards relating to the performance of these products or the coatings used. Where necessary, reference is normally made to the appropriate DIN Standard. However, it has been established that many of the European Standards or drafts have been published by the national body: NEN EN 10169-1; NEN EN 10169-2; NEN EN 508-1; NEN EN 508-2; NEN EN 508-3; NEN EU 169. (Details of the English text of these Standards can be found elsewhere in this report.)

3.1.3. Germany

Site visits

Contact was made with a number of German trade associations and research bodies, including an organisation said to represent the interests of German coil-coating companies, but none were able to cooperate to any great degree with this work (only one questionnaire was completed and returned as discussed in Section 3.1.1 above).

Discussions were held with a German architect, specialising in roof design, who expressed the opinion that approximately 80% of the cladding and roofing installed in Germany is polyester-coated galvanised steel, with the bulk of the remaining 20% comprising polyester- or PVF_2-coated aluminium. The major attraction of the polyester product is its low price. A ten year warranty is commonly given.

It is common practice in Germany to design roof structures without the use of purlins, as is standard UK practice. Main frame columns and beams are spaced at approximately 5 m centres and roofing sheets are profiled to 135 mm–150 mm depth and fixed directly to the beams. The additional depth of profile (compared to typical UK practice) confers the necessary strength and rigidity to cover the increased span.

The major failure found in service is cut edge corrosion. A second common problem is inadequate design of insulation and detailing leading to problems with internal condensation in extreme weather conditions in winter.

Site visits were carried out to a variety of installations accompanied by the architect, as summarised in Table 25.

Table 25. Sites in Germany

Site ref.	Area	Construction	Materials	Comments
G1	Airport terminal building — approximately twenty four years old	Composite panels with secret fixing	Powder-coated aluminium	Some colour variation thought to be the result of panels being replaced following physical damage. Generally very good condition. Other buildings were examined showing signs of edge corrosion, flaking and delamination but neither the age nor nature of the products involved could be determined.
G2	Industrial building near airport — approximately twenty years old	Single-skin cladding with through fixing	Galvanised steel substrate. Coating not known. Given the heavy duty nature of the business, probably a low specification.	Signs of severe physical damage through impact and abrasion, leading to loss of coating and corrosion of substrate. Further corrosion and limited delamination at edges. The coating was chalking badly and showed uneven colour retention.
G3	Various industrial units near Dusseldorf — thought to be between twenty and thirty years old	Mainly single-skin constructions with through fixings	Thought to be mainly steel substrates. Coatings not known.	Serious discolouration (blues worse than reds and browns). Heavy impact damage in some cases, leading to corrosion of the exposed substrate. Also edge and lap corrosion.
G4	Industrial building in rural area — six years old	Single-skin roofing and cladding with through fixing	Polyester-coated galvanised steel. Roof protected with external PVC membrane.	The cladding showed signs of edge corrosion and dirt retention. The PVC roof membrane had failed and was being replaced.
G5	Leisure building in rural area — five years old	Single-skin roofing with secret fixing	Plastisol-coated galvanised steel	Edge corrosion and delamination of coating. Some dirt retention as a result of lack of maintenance.
G6	Industrial building in rural area — seven years old	Composite cladding single-skin roofing	Polyester-coated galvanised steel cladding. Roof protected with external PVC membrane.	Edge corrosion and delamination of cladding and general delamination of cladding and flashings. Also some dirt retention.
G7	Public building in rural area — one year old	Composite cladding and roofing with secret fix	Polyester-coated galvanised steel	Very good condition throughout
G8	Industrial building in rural area — seven years old	Composite panel cladding and built-up composite roofing, both with through fixing	Polyester-coated aluminium. Stainless steel fixings.	Very good condition throughout
G9	Industrial building in rural area — two years old	Secret-fix roofing system	Uncoated aluminium	Very good condition throughout

Table 25. Continued

Site ref.	Area	Construction	Materials	Comments
G10	Industrial building in rural area — eleven years old	Composite panel cladding with secret fixing; single-skin roofing with through fixing	Polyester-coated galvanised steel cladding. Roof coating not known.	Some dirt retention caused by lack of maintenance but otherwise in very good condition
G11	Industrial building in rural area — ten years old	Built-up composite cladding and single-skin roofing, both with through fixings	Polyester-coated galvanised steel	Inappropriate cladding design causes cold bridging and condensation during the winter months. Otherwise performing very well.
G12	Industrial building in urban area close to river — eleven years old	Single-skin cladding with through fixing	Galvanised steel substrate. Coating not known.	Overall loss of colour and gloss
G13	Commercial building in urban area close to river — ten years old	Single-skin cladding with through fixing	Galvanised steel substrate. Coating not known.	Edge corrosion, loss of colour and impact damage

Standards

There exists an extremely wide range of national German Standards relating to the topic under consideration. The most significant is the DIN 55928 series which is summarised in Table 26.

Taken together, the DIN 55928 series can be seen to comprehensively cover the use of coated steel. It contains far more information than the proposed European Standards (EN 10169-1 and EN 10169-2) on continuously organic-coated (coil-coated) steel flat products, which are to be published in Germany as DIN EN 10169-1 and DIN EN 10169-2.

Compliance with the requirements of DIN 55928 Part 8 is a requirement for the awarding of a Ü Mark for products of this type.

The European Standard on coil-coated aluminium has been published as DIN EN 1396.

Some idea of the extent of existing German Standards and other documents in this product area can be gained by examination of DIN 55928 Part 5, which references a total of 40 documents in the text and also lists another 11 documents as being relevant to the product area. No useful purpose would be served by reproducing all of these Standards in this report, but some of the more significant standards relating to the use of coated steel and aluminium are given in Table 27 as an illustration. Numerous other guidelines, codes of practice and other documents of varying degrees of relevance to this work exist.

3.1.4. France

Site visits
Visits were made to two French coil-coating companies.

France commonly accepts a lower galvanising weight than other countries in Europe ($200\,\mathrm{g\,m^{-2}}$, while $275\,\mathrm{g\,m^{-2}}$ is usual in the UK).

Table 26. German Standard DIN 55928

DIN 55928 Protection of steel structures from corrosion by organic and metallic coatings

Part 1 General information, definitions, corrosion factors
Contains basic specifications for the protection of steel structures from corrosion by organic and metallic coatings. Several basic concepts are defined and information is given on corrosion in different media (e.g. air, soil, water). Different atmospheric classes are defined.

Part 2 Design principles for inhibiting corrosion

Contains information on design principles and good practice

Part 3 Planning of corrosion protection procedures
Includes information on initial corrosion protection and on subsequent maintenance

Part 4 Surface preparation and testing of surfaces
Contains specifications for surface protection including definitions of grades of prepared surfaces. This is supported by a photographic appendix.

Part 5 Coating materials and protective systems
Contains information on organic and inorganic coating materials for effective and economic protection of steel structures from corrosion. The constituent parts of such organic systems, such as resins, pigments, etc. are discussed in some detail and specifications are given for inorganic coatings applied by hot-dip galvanising, thermal spraying and electro-galvanising. In addition, typical examples of proven corrosion protection systems are given for various internal and external atmospheres.

Part 6 Execution and inspection of corrosion protection work
Relates to the workmanship and inspection of corrosion protection work. Does not describe the preparation and testing of the substrates, which is covered in Part 4 described above. However, the application method and testing of both coating systems and individual coating layers are specified.

Part 7 Reference areas
Describes the preparation of test areas, the number of which is required is dependent on the structure and on the design of the corrosion protection system

Part 8 Protection of supported thin-walled building components from corrosion
This document describes the corrosion protection of up to 3 mm thick steel used in structurally supported sections and exposed to atmospheric corrosion. The sheets are either galvanised or zinc alloy coated with a supplementary coil coating. The Standard gives information on requirements for substrate, coating materials, application and thickness, surface preparation and design (largely by reference to other published standards). Test methods and requirements are given and a system of manufacturing surveillance is defined.

Part 9 Composition of binders and pigments for coating materials
Gives information on binders and pigments as well as notes for their analytical testing. The mass fraction of corrosion-inhibiting pigments is specified for coatings intended for use as primers and edge protection materials.

Table 27. Relevant German Standards

DIN 267 Part 9 Fasteners; technical delivery conditions; electroplated components
DIN 267 Part 10 Fasteners; technical delivery conditions; hot-dip galvanised components
DIN 267 Part 11 Fasteners; technical delivery conditions; stainless and acid-resistant steel components
DIN 4102 Series Fire behaviour of building materials and building components
DIN 8565 Corrosion protection of steel structures by thermal spray coating with zinc and aluminium; general principles
DIN 17162 Part 1 Hot-dip galvanised mild unalloyed steel sheet and strip; technical delivery conditions*
DIN 17162 Part 2 Hot-dip galvanised general purpose structural steel sheet and strip; technical delivery conditions*
DIN 18516-1 Back-ventilated, non-loadbearing, external enclosures of buildings; requirements and testing.
DIN 18338 Contract procedures for building works — Part C; general technical specifications for building works; roof covering
   and roof sealing works
DIN 50 902 Layers of corrosion protection for metals; definitions, procedures and surface preparation
DIN 50 976 Corrosion protection by means of hot-dip galvanising; requirements and testing
DIN 53 230 Testing paints, varnishes and other coating materials; evaluation system for assessing test results

The European Standards for zinc–aluminium and aluminium–zinc alloy coated steel have been published in Germany as DIN
EN 10214 and DIN EN 10215 respectively

There are many other relevant German documents including:
ALZ A 1 Aluminium roof coverings and wall linings
ALZ A 7 Guidelines for the laying of aluminium profiles
DIN — Fachbericht 35 General requirements for a discontinuously laid roof covering
ZVSHK Fachregeln, Kempner Guidelines for the fabrication of metal roof decks, metal external wall linings and building
   plumbing — Trade-specific rules of sheet meal work
BFS Merkblatt No 6 Painted aluminium building components
MB Stahl 325 Organic pre-coated sheet steel
IFD Aussenwandbekleidungen IFD recommendations for the cladding of external walls with large format building components
KTBL 2030 Structures; structural design; thermally insulated facade linings
DIN 18515 EErl HA Technical Building Regulations; claddings
DNV BTI 1.5 Facade lining
AGK — Arbeitsblatt B1 Testing of metal-plus-paint systems for corrosion protection of steel structures by hot-dip galvanising
   and painting.

*The German versions of the European Standards for such products have also been published as DIN EN 10142 and DIN EN
10147.

'Lead-free galvanising' (95:5% zinc:aluminium) is now commonly used, driven by environmental considerations. These figures refer to inhabited buildings and lower coating weights will be used for constructions such as agricultural buildings.

Recent ECCA figures indicate that 65% of coatings used in construction are polyesters, with 30% being plastisol. It should be noted that the latter is applied at a greatly increased thickness and so the area of installed sheet is considerably lower. Exports of French coated steel to the UK market are primarily plastisol, but this is very rarely used in southern parts of Europe because of concerns over UV resistance in areas of high exposure and perceived environmental considerations. It may be used where special requirements exist, such as where a higher chemical resistance is necessary. PVF_2 is also exported to the UK and is considered probably the best coating available, but is uncommon in France because of its relatively high cost. Two current Agrément Certificates exist for coil-coated materials manufactured in France but marketed in the UK.

Polyesters are the most popular coating system in France, particularly the more recently developed 'superdurable' variety. In addition to the superior top-coat used in such systems, they also use an improved primer coat than earlier equivalents and are considered to have improved formability and UV and corrosion resistance.

It was said that warranty requirements vary from one country to another. One of the coil coaters contacted operates a similar system to that encountered in the UK, where the guarantee period is set depending on the use (i.e. roofing or cladding), colour chosen and direction faced. This warranty is offered for products imported into the UK by the roll former, which is part of the same parent company. The edge corrosion is limited under the warranty to 10 mm edge creep after ten years.

Sites were visited in association with three coil coaters contacted as part of this work. The findings are summarised in Table 28.

Standards
There is a wide range of French Standards relevant to roofing and cladding. The national French Standards identified as particularly relevant are given in Table 29.

The two coated aluminium Standards in the NF P 34-206 series in Table 29 were examined for comparison with the German DIN 55928 series. Part 1 describes the aluminium substrate, two classes of coatings, thermosetting (which are said to be polyester and silicone–polyester) and thermoplastics (plastisol and PVF_2). It gives basic recommendations for the use of the two types, and of uncoated aluminium, depending on the corrosivity of the atmosphere to be encountered.

Information is also given in the materials section of this standard on fixings and other ancillary items and details of transport and storage. The major part of the standard deals with a comprehensive installation and detailing guide. Finally, in a series of appendixes are given maintenance instructions, a corrosivity map of France and further technical information on ventilation, fixings, etc.

Part 2 of the standard is a brief document which has sections on the administration of the work, including the necessary planning and documentation. As with the German Standards, there are a large number of supporting documents, for example NF P 34-206-1 lists in Appendix D a total of 27 other standards referred to in the main text.

Table 28. Sites in France

Site ref.	Area	Construction	Materials	Comments
F1	Industrial building near airport — ten years old	Composite panel cladding	Polyester-coated aluminium	Some impact damage but generally performing very well
F2	Industrial building close to motorway — four years old	Composite cladding with through fixing	Polyester-coated aluminium	Cases of bad workmanship including swarf staining and poor detailing leading to dirt retention and staining. Poor condition for age but no inherent material failures.
F3	Industrial building in area of low pollution — one year old	Single-skin cladding with through fixing	Polyester-coated aluminium	Poor design and workmanship including badly aligned sheets, gaps between overlying sheets, lack of sealing washers for fixings. No inherent material problems.
F4	Industrial building near airport — five years old	Composite cladding with both through and secret fixings. Front elevation pitched at approx 75°.	Polyester-coated aluminium	Some staining and dirt retention apparently caused by detailing/design, principally run off from black glazing gasket and exacerbated by lack of maintenance.
F5	Leisure building in a rural area — seven years old	Single-skin roofing with through fixing	Polyester-coated aluminium	Some corrosion at edges and slight staining caused by poor detailing. Generally very good appearance.
F6	Industrial building in urban area — six years old	Built-up composite cladding and roofing	PVF_2-coated aluminium	Some dirt retention as a result of lack of maintenance. Otherwise very good condition.
F7	Various industrial buildings on rural sites of various ages	Single-skin cladding and roofing with through fixing	PVF_2- and silicone–polyester-coated aluminium	PVF_2 product performing very well after up to four years apart from one area of very localised colour loss — reason not known. Silicone–polyester found to perform well for ten years but faded rapidly thereafter.
F8	Industrial building in very aggressive location — eighteen years old	Single-skin cladding and roofing with through fixing	PVF_2 and silicone–polyester-coated galvanised steel	Edge and lap corrosion, impact damage, chalking and dirt retention. Cracking and consequent corrosion at bends of profiles.

In addition the European Standards covered earlier in this report are being published as national standards.

3.1.5. Scandinavia

There are a number of major manufacturers of coil coatings (and metallic substrates) in Scandinavia and these materials are imported into the UK in significant quantities. No discussions were held with these manufacturers as part of this work, although a number of building research organisations were sent postal questionnaires. The BBA has had dealings with several of these companies in the past and current Agrément Certificates exist for both aluminium–zinc alloy coated steel, and coil-coated steel and aluminium produced in Scandinavia. As part of the assessment leading to the issue of these Certificates, a number of site visits were carried out, as summarised in Table 30.

The Norwegian Building Research Institute (NBI) has published research into the performance of profiled metal roofing in Norway,[103] an English summary of the Norwegian NBI Report 100, and a field survey of and recommended actions for the corrosion protection of metallic fasteners.[104] The former paper describes a study of 75 roofs — 56 steel and 19 aluminium — mainly in coastal areas but also with examples of industrial and rural installations. The ages ranged from new to 15 years. Of the 56 steel roofs, 36 were found to be suffering from corrosion, 33 of which related (but not exclusively) to cut edges. Spot checks indicated that in some cases the galvanizing was well below the specified thickness. Mechanical damage was reported on 25 steel roofs and five aluminium roofs. A variety of problems with workmanship were noted, particularly where the roofs were penetrated, for example, by vents or chimneys. Side laps were often inadequately formed and end laps incorrectly detailed. Problems were also indicated for fixings, leading to a recommendation that only stainless steel screws (not nails) should be used.

Of the 14 double-skinned roofs investigated, eight were found to leak. The problems were assigned to poor workmanship rather than material problems — the report concludes that 'It is obvious that many roofing workers in Norway (and probably also in other countries) lack fundamental knowledge about the trade. The building industry has to do something about it.'

The work on fasteners deals with a variety of products for use in different situations, but includes a section on self-drilling screws for

Table 29. Relevant French Standards

P34-310 Continuously hot-dip zinc-coated structural steel sheet and strip for building purposes. Classification and test.

P34-301 Hot-dip zinc-coated steel sheet and strip either coil coated or organic film laminated for building purposes. Classification and tests.

DTU P 34-205, DTU 40.35 Technical specifications for roof coverings with ribbed plates made from pre-painted or unpainted galvanised steel sheets, contract — special clauses

NF P 34-206-1, DTU 40,36 Building works. Profiled roof covering made of pre-painted or unpainted aluminium sheet. Part 1 Technical specifications

NF P 34-206-2, DTU 40.36 Building Works — Private contracts — profiled roof coverings made of pre-painted aluminium sheet or aluminium sheet. Part 2 special clauses

DTU P 34-201 DTU 40.32 Contract bill for metal corrugated sheet roofing, contract bill of the special clauses

NF P 34-401 Roofing. Ribbed sheets made from galvanised steel either pre-painted or unpainted. Dimensional characteristics.

NF T 30-808 Paints and varnishes for civil engineering and building activities. Guide relating to paint products and systems for facades. Mineral coatings, organic coatings.

NF A 50-452 Aluminium and aluminium alloys. Coil coating strip and sheet. Characteristics.

Table 30. Sites in Scandinavia

Site ref.	Area	Construction	Materials	Comments
S1	Industrial building— twelve years old	Cladding	PVF$_2$-coated galvanised steel	Very good condition throughout
S2	Industrial building— 21 years old	Cladding	PVF$_2$- and polyester-coated aluminium	Severe impact damage. Comparison with standard showed excellent colour retention for PVF$_2$. Polyester faded badly.
S3	Industrial building— ten years old	Cladding	Plastisol-coated galvanised steel	Very good condition overall. Some rusting of retained swarf.
S4	External store— age not known	Cladding	Polyester-coated galvanised steel	Impact damage but very good condition throughout
S5	Industrial building— ten years old	Cladding	PVF$_2$-coated galvanised steel	Impact damage but very good condition throughout
S6	Industrial building— 17 years old	Single-skin cladding with through fixing	Polyester-coated aluminium	Some fading but generally in very good condition
S7	Security hut in industrial location— three years old	Formed tile profiled roof	PVF$_2$-coated aluminium	Very good condition throughout
S8	Leisure building in an exposed coastal location— over ten years old	Formed tile profiled roof	PVF$_2$-coated aluminium	Some salt staining but otherwise in very good condition
S9	Industrial building in an exposed coastal location— ten years old	Cladding with through fixing	PVF$_2$-coated aluminium	Same impact damage and salt staining but otherwise in very good condition

steel decks not exposed to external elements. These were included to offer a simple and secure fastening method. Recommendations are made for the required corrosion resistance in given installations based on Kesternich sulphur dioxide testing.

3.1.6. Other European countries

Visits were also made to other sites in Europe as shown in Table 31.

3.2. United States

3.2.1. Industry structure

It was estimated by one American coil coater that the total market for coil-coated products in the United States in 1995 was four million tonnes worth over a billion US dollars (this represents all uses, not only construction).

The National Coil Coaters Association, based in Chicago, may be considered as the American counterpart of the ECCA. It represents the interests of its members by assessing the implications of all legislation and standardisation of coil-coated materials, health and safety issues and generally promotes the industry. Membership of the NCCA stood at 173 in August 1996. The 1995 *Product Capability Directory*[105] breaks the membership down as shown in Table 32.*

It is the responsibility of all members to report their production levels to the NCCA (but not all do). From these statistics a quarterly shipment report is produced which details the production by end use. The first quarter report for 1996 showed that the companies providing information produced approximately 190 000 tonnes of steel and 10 000 tonnes of aluminium for use in cladding and roofing.

The NCCA also has a technical function. It produces a series of publications giving advice on how a customer can become involved in using coil-coated metal and other technical and publicity material. A technical committee has been set up to assess the extent of cut edge corrosion and to investigate possible improvements in this area.

Table 31. Sites elsewhere in Europe

Site ref.	Area	Construction	Materials	Comments
E1	Industrial building in rural Switzerland — newly completed	Single-skin cladding with through fixing	Polyester-coated aluminium	Some impact damage but generally performing well
E2	Ferry terminal, Belgium — thirteen years old	Cladding with through fixing	Aluminium substrate. Coating not known.	Loss of colour and gloss, chalking and salt staining caused by very aggressive environment. Maintenance schedule not known.

Table 32. Membership of the National Coil Coaters Association

	United States	Europe	Other
Coil coaters	38	4	16
Adhesive suppliers	2	1	1
Chemical suppliers	18	0	1
Coating suppliers	24	5	4
Machinery/equipment	15	0	2
Metal suppliers	17	0	3
Other suppliers	3	0	0

*The directory lists only those companies that wish to be included and does not represent the whole industry.

3.2.2. Survey results

Discussions were held with two of the three American coil coaters contacted, three major coating suppliers and two leading construction companies.

There are no nationally recognised American specifications or standards for the manufacture and use of organically coated metals in construction. Most individual states have their own regional building codes, largely based on the specific state climate, (as an example, the pH of rain on the East coast has been measured as low as 2.1 — this situation is not paralleled on the West coast, where the major atmospheric problem is high UV radiation), geography and accepted local construction techniques. The materials easily available locally also have an influence. Each state usually requires verification that a specified system is suitable for its intended use from an independent third party assessor. This involves ASTM (American Society for Testing and Materials) test methods, but the interpretation of results would be based on the known local conditions.

American coil coaters operate primarily as toll coaters as discussed in Section 1.1.2 of this report. In order to regulate quality control, one major building system manufacturer sets specifications for the coated product, carries out comprehensive fitness testing prior to accepting a product and then tests each batch of material supplied. In this way almost the same level of control can be exercised as over production in-house.

Galvanised steel is the most commonly used substrate, normally in G90* grade. The G60† grade may be used in the agricultural sector where durability requirements are lower. Problems have been reported in the past with formability after zinc phosphate pretreatments but modern pretreatment methods have overcome this. Aluminium is usually restricted to prestigious developments, coastal areas or other locations in corrosive environments.

Aluminium–zinc (55:45) alloy coated steel has been used as a substrate for coil coating in the past and continues to be available but problems have been reported with edge corrosion and coating delamination. The use of this material is now largely restricted to uncoated applications in low-pitched roofing systems, including standing seam, and there is an established 20-year history of satisfactory service in this condition.

It is generally accepted in the United States that the 70:30 PVF_2–acrylic is the preferred coating system. It can be applied at varying thicknesses depending on the corrosivity of the environment in which it is to be installed. Polyester coatings are second in popularity to PVF_2

*Equivalent to Z275.
†Equivalent to Z185.

and are probably more often used. The modern polyesters are considered as being very close in performance to the PVF_2 but remain lower in price. Some thin coat PVCs (organosols) were installed in the 1960s, but problems were encountered with lack of UV resistance in the extreme conditions encountered in certain areas of the US. As a result PVCs have not been used for a number of years and so there is no experience of the modern thicker formulated plastisols currently available.

One of the major coil coaters contacted stated that their production consisted of 85% polyesters, 10% PVF_2 and 5% speciality coatings, but this represents one company only and may not accurately reflect the industry as a whole.

At least one company is working towards introducing a powder coil-coating line at some point in the future. The policy of toll coating introduces another step into the production chain as discussed in Section 1.1.2. However, from the limited discussions held it would appear that efforts are made by the system manufacturers and suppliers to ensure that specifications are rigidly defined and adhered to. Warranties of 20 years are offered by the system producers for the PVF_2 product in partnership with the coaters and coating and substrate suppliers. This covers the product for film integrity, fading and chalking. A reduced warranty may be offered for cheaper products. It was stated by one of the coil coaters that claims in 1995 amounted to less than 1% of all production. This company was hoping to be assessed against ISO 9002 by the end of 1996, which it was said would reduce the release of faulty products still further. (In general the registration of firms to the ISO 9000 Series appears to be less advanced than in Europe.)

3.2.3. Site visits

Given the wide climatic variations to be found across the US, it is not surprising that coating companies use a number of exposure sites in different locations throughout the country. A visit was made to a Florida exposure site operated by one of the coating manufacturers and data were examined from a second such site.

On the site examined, samples were produced from G90 galvanised steel, aluminium – zinc alloy coated steel and aluminium, the oldest of which had been exposed for 24 years. They are exposed at 45° and 5° South. Each new product or pigment/colour change must successfully complete a five-year exposure before acceptance. Of the samples examined, the PVF_2 generally had the best performance, with older acrylics and PVCs showing signs of failure.

Examination of the site records and publicity material indicates that records kept on the site climate are comprehensive and similar to those previously encountered in European exposure sites. This means that the performance of the coatings can be closely matched to the conditions experienced. One way of accelerating the process further is by focusing solar energy onto the samples using a system of mirrors; at least two such systems are known to be in operation in Florida and Arizona.

Sites visited and the contacts made during this work are listed in Table 33.

3.2.4. Standards

There are no known International (ISO) Standards dealing directly with organically coated metals for use in construction although standards do exist for wrought aluminium and aluminium alloy sheets, strips and plates (ISO 6361 Parts 1–4), on continuous hot-dip zinc coated carbon steel sheet of structural quality (ISO 4998) and work is progressing under Technical Committee ISE/10 towards a similar document for continuous hot-dip zinc – 5% aluminium alloy coated steel sheet. Other related standards cover the testing of substrates and paints, components of paint systems such as pigments, binders and solvents, fixings, the preparation of steel surfaces prior to painting and the mechanical testing (such as simulated wind pressure, snow loading, etc.) of structures.

As described above there is no national standard used to provide a specification for coil coatings in the United States. An examination of the published standards has been made and the principal standard that has been identified relating to the products under consideration is ASTM A 755/A 755 M Steel sheet, metallic coated by the hot-dip process and pre-painted by the coil-coating process for exterior exposed building products.

ASTM A755 is a limited standard which gives ordering information and details of mechanical requirements, dimensions and tolerances, pretreatment, coating systems, test methods and packaging. The standard contains little detail and contains a number of references to other relevant standards, particularly for test methods. It gives a list of typical coating systems such as polyester, silicone polyester, acrylic, silicone modified acrylic, fluoropolymers, organosol and laminated films, but no recommendations as to suitable areas of use.

Of the test methods specified as requirements, four are ASTM methods (D522 Conical mandrel, D523 Gloss, D2244 Colour and D3363 Film hardness) but the remaining three (Dry film thickness, Cure test and U bend), are to be agreed between the producer and purchaser. A further six tests — B117 Salt spray, D659 Weatherometer, D822 Artificial Weathering, D870 Water immersion, D1735 Water fog and D2247

Table 33. Sites in the United States

Site ref.	Area	Construction	Materials	Comments
US1	Industrial building in Chicago — twenty one years old	Composite cladding with through fixing	PVF_2-coated galvanised steel	Some evidence of dirt retention (no routine maintenance), impact damage and minor edge corrosion at bottom of sheets. Generally very good condition.
US2	Commercial building in industrial area of Chicago — twenty years old	Cladding thought to be of composite construction	Thought to be PVF_2 coating. Substrate not known.	Some dirt retention and lap corrosion (no routine maintenance). Generally very good condition.
US3	Sheltered leisure building in Chicago — thirteen years old	Roofing and cladding thought to be of composite construction	PVF_2-coated galvanized steel	Edge and lap corrosion promoted by high levels of internal moisture being discharged at soffits. Otherwise very good condition.
US4	Industrial building in aggressive location in Chicago — twenty two years old	Single-skin cladding with through fixing	PVF_2-coated galvanized steel. One elevation overcoated with a silicone–acrylic in 1988. Another area overcoated with plastisol at the same time.	Cracking of galvanising caused by roll forming and impact damage was noted. Two examples of severe corrosion around incorrectly installed fixings and cases of lap and edge corrosion. PVF_2 coating showed good colour retention and the acrylic was also performing well. However, the plastisol area showed chalking and poor colour retention.
US5	Various industrial buildings in aggressive Chicago locations — approximately thirty years old	Details not known (mainly steel substrates)	Details not known	A wide range of failures were noted, including rusting caused by embedded swarf, some edge corrosion but no major substrate failure. The most common problem was severe and uneven colour loss.
US6	Leisure building in coastal Florida — fourteen years old	Composite panel cladding with secret fixings	Commercial multicoat 225 μm system (metallic finish)	Some impact damage but generally in very good condition
US7	Commercial building in central Chicago — approximately five years old	Composite panel cladding with secret fixing	PVF_2 finish, substrate not known	Excellent condition — no faults noted
US8	Leisure building in urban Chicago — three years old	Single-skin roofing and composite in-fill panels in concrete structure. Secret fix and standing seam constructions	PVF_2-coated G90 galvanised steel	Initial impressions indicated excellent condition. Closer examination showed edge corrosion and delamination on certain panels.

Table 33. Continued

Site ref.	Area	Construction	Materials	Comments
US9	Industrial building in Chicago — eleven years old	Composite in-fill panels and cladding	PVF_2-coated galvanised steel	Minor edge corrosion and differential fading. The latter was caused by the use of two different products on one elevation and was said to have been accepted at the time of construction.
US10	Industrial building located near Chicago — ten years old	Composite panels and cladding with secret fixing	PVF_2-coated galvanised steel	Very good condition throughout
US11	Industrial building located near Chicago — ten years old	Composite panels and cladding with secret fixing	PVF_2-coated galvanised steel	Some cracking of coating caused by forming and a very small amount of edge corrosion. One case of sealant failure. Generally in good condition.
US12	Various industrial buildings near Chicago — approximtely eleven years old	Mainly standing-seam constructions	Full details not known — thought to be mainly galvanised steel with either polyester or PVF_2 coatings	Examples of edge corrosion including one case of delamination, rusting caused by embedded swarf, and one case of discolouration caused by chemical contamination
US13	Shopping mall in Chicago — approximately eleven years old	Roofing	Aluminium substrate. Coating unknown.	Very good appearance with no faults visible
US14	Industrial building near Chicago — ten years old	Composite cladding with secret fixing	Silicone-polyester-coated galvanised steel	Limited edge corrosion and slight evidence of cracking at roll-formed edges

Humidity — are optional and two further tests (D714 Degree of Blistering and D1654 Painted specimens subjected to corrosive environments) are given for performance evaluation. Associated standards (excluding the numerous test methods) are given in Table 34.

Of the galvanising standards described in Table 34, A 525 gives information on finishes, manufacture, requirements for delivery, chemical and mechanical requirements, test methods, dimensions, workmanship and other information. A 446 is intended primarily for steel for use where structural properties are required and so is peripheral to this study, but A 361 is specifically aimed at cladding and roofing use. In addition to the information given in A 525, it contains specific specifications for chemical composition, coating requirements and dimensions and tolerances. ASTM D 2092 Preparation of zinc-coated (galvanised) steel surfaces for painting and D 1730 Practices for preparation of aluminium and aluminium alloy surfaces for painting are also relevant.

Aluminium substrates are covered by ASTM B 209S Aluminium and Aluminium Alloy Sheet and Plate, although no parallel standard to A 755, to cover coil-coated aluminium, appears to exist.

Two further standards exist with potential implications for the repair of coil coatings or the overcoating of such products at the end of their decorative lives: ASTM D 3276 Standard Guide for Painting Inspectors (Metal Substrates) and ASTM D 4228 Qualification of Coating Applicators for Application of Coatings to Steel Surfaces. The former gives guidance on surface preparation and inspection and the latter provides a standard qualifying method for coating applicators to verify their proficiency and ability to achieve the required quality for the application of specified coatings to steel surfaces. (No such formal standard is known to exist in Europe.)

The ASTM currently publish a vast number of standard test methods for paints, many of which could be considered to be relevant to this work and some of which are called up in European Standards for coated steel and aluminium. Some of the more significant have already been discussed; others are given in Table 35.

Furthermore, ASTM D 3451 Standard practices for testing polymeric powders and powder coatings specifies 36 test methods and nine other standard specifications. ASTM D 3794 Standard guide for testing coil-coatings specifies 52 ASTM test methods/practices and 15 National Coil Coater Standard test methods as published by the National Coil Coaters Association.

Table 34. *Relevant American galvanising standards*

ASTM A 361/A 361 M Zinc coated (galvanised) by the hot-dip process for roofing and siding
ASTM A 525/A 525 M Standard specification for general requirements for steel sheet, zinc coated (galvanised) by the hot-dip process
ASTM A 446/A 446 M Standard specification for steel sheet, zinc coated (galvanised) by the hot-dip process, structural (physical) quality

Table 35. *Relevant American test standards*

ASTM C 481 Standard test method for laboratory ageing of sandwich constructions
ASTM D 660 Standard test method for evaluating degree of chalking of exterior paints
ASTM D 3363 Standard test method for film hardness by pencil test
ASTM D 4145 Standard test method for coating flexibility of pre-painted sheet
ASTM D 4214 Standard test methods for evaluating the degree of chalking for exterior paint films
ASTM G 85 Standard practice for modified salt spray fog testing

In addition to the above, the American Architectural Manufacturers Association have published a number of relevant documents including the following.

(*a*) Standard specifications for aluminium siding, soffit and fascia, which covers coated and uncoated materials and includes test methods and performance criteria for wind loading and impact resistance, requirements for the aluminium substrate, coatings (including test methods that are mainly, but not exclusively, ASTM based), fasteners and installation (by reference to the Aluminium Association's Aluminium Siding Application Manual).

(*b*) Voluntary specification for high performance organic coatings on architectural aluminium extrusions and panels. This covers only factory spray applied coatings and gives some general information, including metal pretreatment, but is primarily concerned with test methods.

3.3. Australasia

Questionnaires were sent to two organisations known to be active in research in this area — CSIRO (Commonwealth Scientific and Industrial Research Organisation) of Australia and BRANZ (Building Research Association of New Zealand). The replies can be found in Appendix 2.

CSIRO is conducting an exposure research programme on these materials.[106,107] A number of coated products from five countries, including acrylic, polyester, silicone–polyesters, PVF_2 and PVC and PVF laminates on steels and aluminium, together with uncoated samples of mild steel, low alloy copper steel, zinc and both 5:95% and 55:45% aluminium–zinc alloy coated steel, have been exposed on three marine sites in Australia. The samples were installed not only in the open, but also in a glass shelter designed to minimise change to the climatic environment while permitting deposition of airborne salt and particles, but preventing washing by rainwater. A methodology has been developed (but not yet published) to quantify the defects found for each of the specimens. The project is due for completion in 1998 or 1999, but the early results indicate that the sheltered corrosion rates are approximately seven times those in the open, the 55:45% aluminium–zinc alloy sample showing the lowest corrosion rate of the uncoated materials, which on average is one-third of that experienced by zinc.

The BRANZ publication *Guidelines for the technical assessments of coil-coated products*[108] is intended to provide assistance in carrying out detailed technical assessments of these products for building purposes. It is largely in the format of a check list covering all aspects of product specification and handling to ensure that it is appropriate for its intended use. Information is also given on aluminium grades, colour variation and limits and on test methods and requirements. BRANZ has awarded Approval Certificates for organically coated metal cladding and roofing products.

A number of other BRANZ publications[109-111] deal with areas of interest. Further work has been carried out (but not completed) to investigate the overcoating of weathered coil coatings. This work demonstrated that adhesion of the overcoating system to older PVF_2 formulations could be problematic, but this was reported to be significantly improved with more modern PVF_2 formulations. Similar investigations of the overcoating of rusted galvanised steel are expected to be reported in the near future.

No other investigations into the use of these materials in Australasia were carried out for this report.

3.4. Conclusions

The major materials suppliers are multi-national companies and coated products are widely exported by manufacturers to other countries and, indeed, continents. As a result there is a commonality of the products and technology freely available. Despite this, the dominant materials specified differ between countries (and, in the United States, possibly between individual states) largely based on the regional climate but also on traditional preferences and, perhaps increasingly, environmental pressures (for example, PVC, hexavalent chromium). The most commonly used coating system in the United Kingdom, plastisol, is also widely accepted in Northern Europe for its high corrosion resistance, but is unpopular in areas with high levels of UV radiation, where polyesters or PVF_2 are favoured. There is less variation in substrates, with galvanised steel being the most widespread and aluminium being specified most often for prestigious projects or for use in areas of high corrosivity. Some conflict appears to exist as to the suitability of aluminium–zinc alloy coated steel as a base for coil coatings; while this is fully accepted in the United Kingdom, there is some resistance abroad, particularly in the United States (where this material is used substantially without an organic coating).

The performance of these materials has recently begun to be guaranteed by the manufacturer. The details of these warranties show some variation between companies but in general the period of cover is longer in the UK, as a result of a combination of the product covered, low UV climate and definition of failure. No latent defect insurance schemes have been identified overseas; this is not to say that these could not become available should the demand exist.

Insufficient data are available from this study to enable any rigorous statistical analysis to be made of the modes of failure of cladding and roofing outside the UK. It is only possible to form general impressions from the discussions and visits made. However, the most common form of failure in the United Kingdom has previously been shown[3,16] to be cut edge corrosion and subsequent delamination of the coating. This is also a major problem in the countries visited, where different coating systems are usually employed. The problem is often exacerbated by a lack of training of the workforce leading to poor on-site workmanship and bad practice, failure of the building occupant to carry out routine maintenance and, on occasions, poor initial design and detailing of the building. An additional problem, not commonly reported in the UK, is the cracking of galvanising during profiling leading to subsequent failure of the coating at this point. Since the flexibility of both organic and inorganic coatings is well known, this must be assigned to problems with the manufacture of the coil or inappropriate forming techniques/profiles for a given combination of materials.

As referred to above, the nature of the coil coating industry means that the products and technology available do not vary significantly world-wide. There are differences in procedures (for example, the prevalence of toll coating in the US) and in the preferred choice of materials but with the possible exception of cut edge corrosion, the major problems are attributable to design and workmanship on-site rather than faults inherent in the products.

The depth of coverage by national standards varies greatly. It may be noted that Germany, which has a comprehensive range of standards, appears to suffer from the same material problems, although in the limited number of sites visited there appeared fewer cases of poor workmanship than were evident elsewhere in Europe and America. The question of national standards will be addressed by the publication of the European Standards discussed elsewhere in this report and the eventual availability of CE marking. However, these documents will not in themselves improve the quality of design and site practice and are still some way from publication and use.

4. Current and proposed standards

This chapter considers current standards for coated metal roofing and cladding, and describes the work in progress in Europe which will result in the issue of new European and British Standards. The current and proposed standards for substrates, test methods, and the manufacture, properties and installation of coated products are reviewed, including both standards issued through the formal standardisation process and authoritative documents issued by other bodies. The original schedule of work (as detailed in Table 1) required the following elements to be included in this investigation:

4.1 Current test methods
4.2 Recommendations for test methods
4.3 British Standards
4.4 Progress in CEN Standards
4.5 Support for CEN Standards
4.6 Support for Codes of Practice
4.7 Expectations for design life.

However, as these subjects were investigated in the course of the study, it was found that these separate elements were interrelated. For the sake of clarity it was considered more appropriate to present the information in the form given in this chapter than to use the structure proposed originally.

4.1. Background to standardisation

Traditionally, the materials used in buildings and the techniques for their application were the subjects of British Standards and Codes of Practice. As trade in building materials increased, International and European Standards increased in importance, BSI undertook (as one of its obligations as a member of CEN) to issue new European Standards as British Standards and to withdraw any competing British Standard, and reduced its emphasis on national standards work.

Originally, BSI's policy was to give International and European Standards dual or triple numbering (for example, BS 5750: Part 1: 1987, ISO 9001: 1987, EN 29001: 1987). They have now discontinued this practice and introduced the BS ISO and BS EN series, which preserve the original number of the International or European Standard (for example BS ISO 9000 or BS EN 485).

BSI had previously decided to discontinue the Code of Practice series and to issue such codes in the General series of publications. Consequently, there are a number of separate series of British Standards, as described in Table 36.

4.2. Review of standards

4.2.1. General

The standards from these series which are relevant to coated metals have been identified and are listed in Tables 37 to 40. The standards listed include specifications for substrates, coatings and coated metal; test methods for coatings and coated metal; guidance on design, installation and maintenance; relevant standards for colour, fire performance, and for competing materials. The majority of standards listed are current, but withdrawn standards are listed if they describe a test method which is still in use, a material that is still specified, or to show the background to standards which have been revised and reissued.

Standards from the general series are listed in Table 37, those from the CP and PD series in Table 39, and standards from the BS EN and BS ISO series in Table 40. Table 38 details the relationship between BS 3900, International and European Standards.

Some current work in this field is conducted by ISO, but the majority is being conducted by CEN—this work (and the British Standards committees which are handling it) is described in Table 41. Any purely national work is to extend the scope of an existing standard, and is described under that standard in Table 37.

Table 36. Explanation of series of British Standards

Series	Scope
General	All purely national British Standards issued to date. International and European Standards adopted as British Standards before the BS ISO and BS EN series were introduced. Codes of Practice issued since 1975
CP Codes of Practice	Codes of Practice for installation and design, issued up to 1974
PD Published Documents	Guidance document, which may be incomplete or tentative, and does not have the status of a Standard
BS ISO	Current procedure for ISO Standards adopted as British Standards
BS EN	Current procedure for European Standards adopted as British Standards
BS EN ISO	Current procedure for ISO Standards adopted as European Standards and issued as British Standards

Table 37. British Standards (General series) relevant to coated metals and related subjects

BS Number	Title	Nature of Standard	Commentary
381C: 1996	Specification for colours for identification, coding and special purposes	Recommended range of 91 colours	Originally issued in 1948 as 'Colours for ready mixed paints.' Not used in cladding and roofing industry, which prefers BS 4800, NCS and RAL scales
476	Fire tests on building materials and structures	Fire tests for particular situations	
Part 3: 1958	External fire exposure roof tests	Roof tests	Withdrawn. Quotes AA to DD scale of performance. Building Regulations use this scale, and refer to this edition, despite its 'withdrawn' status Annex E of BS 5427: Part 1 1996 reproduces the text of this 'withdrawn' standard, hence giving it 'current' status
Part 3: 1975	External fire exposure roof test		Current. Expresses time to penetration. Not used in Building Regulations
Part 6: 1989	Methods of test for fire propagation for products	Test for lining/wall	Performance in this test is used with Part 7 to define Class O in Building Regulations
Part 7: 1987	Method for classification of the surface spread of flame of products	Test for lining/wall	Performance in this test is used to define other Classes in Building Regulations
729: 1971	Specification for hot-dip galvanised coatings on iron and steel articles	Specification for galvanised articles	Not appropriate for sheet material
849: 1939	Code of practice for plain sheet zinc roofing	Code of Practice for zinc	Partly replaced by BS 6451: 1985
1178: 1982	Specification for milled lead sheet for building purposes	Specification for lead	To be replaced when pr EN 503 is issued as BS EN 503
1449: Part 2: 1982	Specification for stainless and heat-resisting steel plate, sheet and strip	Specification for stainless steel	
1470: 1987	Specification for wrought aluminium and aluminium alloys for general purposes: plate, sheet and strip	Specification for aluminium	Withdrawn. Replaced by EN 485 Parts 1 to 4, EN 515 and EN 573 Parts 1 to 4
1494: Part 1: 1964	Specification for fixing accessories for building purposes: fixings for sheet, roof and wall coverings	Specification for fixings	Refers also to BS 4174
1615: 1987	Method for specifying anodic oxidation coatings on aluminium and its alloys	Specification for anodised aluminium	
1747:	Methods for measurement of air pollution (13 parts)	Test methods for atmospheric contaminants	

Table 37. Continued

BS Number	Title	Nature of Standard	Commentary
2989: 1992	Specification for continuously hot-dip zinc-coated and iron–zinc alloy coated steel flat products	Specification for galvanised steel sheet	Withdrawn. Replaced by EN 10142, 10143 and 10147
3083: 1988	Specification for hot-dip zinc-coated and hot-dip aluminium–zinc coated corrugated steel sheets for general purposes	Specification for galvanised and AZ-coated corrugated steel sheet	
3855: 1965	Method for modified Erichsen cupping test for sheet and strip metal	Test method for ductility of sheet metal	Equivalent to ISO 8490
3900	Methods of test for paints		Some parts of BS 3900 implement the work of ISO or CEN as British Standards, some parts are dual-numbered, or some parts of BS 3900 have been withdrawn and replaced by standards in the BS EN series (see Table 38) BS 5427: Part 1: 1996 gives a list of paint film properties and recommends that they are tested in accordance with relevant parts of BS 3900
	Group A (18 parts)	Tests on liquid paints (excluding chemical tests)	
	Group B (18 parts)	Chemical tests on liquid paints and paint films	
	Group C (9 parts)	Tests for film formation properties	
	Group D (10 parts)	Optical tests on paint films	
	Group E (13 parts)	Mechanical tests	
	Group F (15 parts)	Durability tests	
	Group G (8 parts)	Environmental tests	
	Group H (6 parts)	Tests for film defects	
	Group J (9 parts)	Tests for powders	
4154: 1985	Corrugated plastics translucent sheets made from thermosetting polyester resin (glass fibre reinforced)	Specification for corrugated GRP sheets	
4174: 1972	Specification for self-tapping screws and metallic drive screws	Specification for fixings	Listed as obsolescent, and partly replaced by EN ISO 1479 and 7049
4203: 1980	Extruded rigid PVC corrugated sheeting	Specification for corrugated PVC sheets	
4300: 1969	Wrought aluminium and aluminium alloys for general engineering purposes (supplementary series)	Specification for aluminium	Parts 6, 7 and 8 (for 3105, 5005 and 5454 alloys) withdrawn and replaced first by BS 1470, then by EN 485, 515 and 573
4313: 1988	Specification for strontium chromate pigments for paints	Specification for anti-corrosive pigment	

Table 37. Continued

BS Number	Title	Nature of Standard	Commentary
4315: 1970 Part 2	Methods of test for resistance to air and water penetration Permeable walling constructions (water penetration)	Methods of test for cladding systems	
4422: Part 1: 1987 Part 2: 1990	Glossary of terms associated with fire General terms and phenomena of fire Structural fire protection	Glossary of fire terms	Standard dual-numbered as ISO 8421
4479: 1990 Part 1 Part 4 Part 6	Design of articles that are to be coated General recommendations Recommendations for paint coatings and varnish coatings Recommendations for hot-dip metal coatings	Recommendations for design of items to be coated	
4800: 1989	Schedule of paint colours for building purposes	Recommended range of 100 colours	Associated with BS 4903, 4904 and 5252
4842: 1984	Specification for liquid organic coatings for application to aluminium alloy extrusions, sheet and preformed sections for external architectural purposes, and for the finish on aluminium alloy extrusions, sheet and preformed sections coated with liquid organic coatings	Specification for coating for aluminium	Subject of current work in CEN TC 139 WG5, (pr EN 12206-2), which will eventually replace it
4868: 1972	Specification for profiled aluminium sheet for building		Covers trapezoidal and sinusoidal profiles
4903: 1979	Specification for external colours for farm buildings	Restricted range of 40 colours	Withdrawn. Incorporated into BS 5502 Part 20: 1990
4904: 1978	Specification for external cladding colours for building purposes	Recommended range of 38 colours	Associated with BS 4800 and 5252
5193: 1991	Specification for zinc phosphate pigments for paints	Specification for anti-corrosive pigments	
5250: 1989	Code of Practice for control of condensation in buildings		
5252: 1976	Framework for colour coordination for building purposes	Defines wide range of 237 colours	BS 4800, 4903 and 4904 give smaller ranges taken from this standard
5427: 1976	Code of Practice for performance and loading criteria for profiled sheeting in building	Code of Practice for design and installation of profiled sheet	Withdrawn. Replaced by BS 5427 Part 1: 1996

Table 37. Continued

BS Number	Title	Nature of Standard	Commentary
5427: Part 1: 1996	Code of Practice for the use of profiled sheet for roof and wall cladding on buildings. Design	Code of Practice for design of profiled sheet installation	Replaces text of BS 5427: 1976 in respect of design (Part 2 on installation is proposed)
5466: Part 7: 1982	Methods for corrosion testing of metallic coatings: guidance on stationary outdoor exposure corrosion tests	Methods for exposure tests on metal coatings	
5502	Buildings and structures for agriculture	General codes for design of agricultural buildings	
Part 20	Code of Practice for general design considerations		Part 20 includes a restricted range of 16 preferred colours and 12 harmonised colours (which were originally in BS 4903)
Part 21	Code of Practice for selection and use of construction materials		Part 21 gives the composition of metal coatings and in effect restates the requirements of BS 3083
Part 22	Code of Practice for design, construction and loading		
5534	Code of Practice for slating and tiling		Appropriate for design of installations using preformed tiles and slates
5750	Quality systems		Main parts replaced by EN ISO 9000 series
5950	Structural use of steelwork in building		
Part 6: 1995	Code of Practice for design of light gauge profiled steel sheeting		Requires structural grades of galvanised steel
Part 7: 1992	Specification for materials and workmanship: cold-formed sections		Requires galvanised or AZ-coated sheet — organic coatings to be specified by designer
6100	Glossary of building and civil engineering terms		
Part 1: Section 1.3.1	Walls and cladding	Glossaries of cladding and roofing terms	
Part 1: Section 1.3.2	Roofs and roofing		
6105: 1981	Specification for corrosion-resistant stainless steel fasteners		Equivalent to ISO 3506; more relevant to industrial uses than building uses
6161	Methods of test for anodic oxidation coatings on aluminium and its alloys		

Table 37. Continued

BS Number	Title	Nature of Standard	Commentary
6399 Part 1: 1984 Part 2: 1995 Part 3: 1988	Loading for buildings Code of Practice for dead and imposed loads Code of Practice for wind loads Code of Practice for imposed roof loads	Fundamental design procedures for buildings	Has replaced CP 3: Chapter V: Part 2 (although this remains current)
6496: 1984	Specification for powder organic coatings for application and stoving to aluminium alloy extrusions, sheet and preformed sections for external architectural purposes, and for the finish on aluminium alloy extrusions, sheet and preformed sections coated with powder organic coatings	Specification for powder coating for aluminium	Subject of current work in CEN TC 139 WG5, (pr EN 12206-1), which will eventually replace it
6497: 1984	Specification for powder organic coatings for application and stoving to hot-dip galvanized hot-rolled steel sections and preformed steel sheet for windows and associated external architectural purposes, and for the finish on galvanized steel sections and preformed sheet coated with powder organic coatings	Specification for powder coating for galvanised steel	Subject of current work in CEN TC 139 WG8, which will eventually replace it
6536: 1985	Specification for continuously hot-dip aluminium – silicon coated cold- reduced carbon steel sheet and strip	Specification for aluminised steel	Withdrawn. Equivalent to ISO 5000 and Euronorm 154, replaced by EN 10154
6561: 1985	Specification for zinc alloy sheet and strip for building	Specification for zinc – titanium and zinc – lead for roofing and flashings	
6582: 1985	Specification for continuously hot-dip lead alloy (terne) coated cold-reduced carbon steel rolled flat products	Specification for terne-coated steel	Equivalent to ISO 4999 and Euronorm 153
6781: 1986	Specification for continuously organic coated steel flat products	Specification for coil-coated steel	Equivalent to Euronorm 169. Withdrawn and replaced by BS EN 10169-1
6915: 1988	Specification for design and construction of fully supported lead sheet roof and wall coverings	Code of Practice for lead roofing and cladding	
6923: 1988	Method for calculation of small colour differences		Modification of CIELAB colour difference procedure
7543: 1992	Guide to durability of buildings and building elements, products and components		

Table 37. Continued

BS Number	Title	Nature of Standard	Commentary
8000	Workmanship on building sites	Guide on workmanship for common building operations	The 15 published parts of this standard do not include metal roofing and cladding
8200: 1985	Code of Practice for design of non-loadbearing external vertical enclosures of buildings	Code for design of curtain walling and panel systems	
8210: 1986	Guide to building maintenance management		Encourages systematic inspection and timely maintenance

Outside the standards process, the desire to promote international trade in building materials has fostered international cooperation by other organisations, and has stimulated national efforts to provide input to this international work. The consequence has been that substantial international agreement has been reached and various authoritative documents have been published, but these have not (or not yet) been published as standards. These publications are listed in Table 42.

4.2.2. Standards for substrates

In the past, coil coatings were applied to galvanised steel sheet to BS 2989 or to aluminium to BS 1470 and 4300 (parts 6, 7 or 8). Substantial European work has taken place on both materials, with the result that galvanised steel is now covered by EN 10142, 10143 and 10147, and aluminium sheet by EN 485, 515 and 573. Parallel work has also been conducted on other coated steels, and standards EN 10154, 10214 and 10215 have been issued for aluminium–silicon and aluminium–zinc (5% and 55% Al) coated steels.

All of the coated steel standards cover a variety of coating weights and steel compositions, in particular the coating weights they include are not all appropriate for external exposure. However, the standards include a designation scheme which allows the steel to be specified precisely, and the standards for coated steel considered below give guidance on the designations which are appropriate for external exposure.

Similarly, the aluminium standards include a variety of aluminium alloy compositions, not all of which are suitable for external exposure. The standards also include a designation scheme, which enables the material to be specified precisely, and the standards for coated aluminium considered below also give guidance on appropriate specifications for external exposure.

Table 38. Relationship between BS 3900, International and European Standards

Part of BS 3900	Equivalent ISO standard	Equivalent EN Standard*
A1	1512	
A2	1513	
A3	1514	605
A6	2431	535
A8	1516	
A9	1523	
A10	3233	
A13	3680	
A14		456
A16	7254	
A17	7877	
A18	9514	
B4	6503	
B5	6713	
B6	3856-1	
B7	3856-2	
B8	3856-3	
B9	3856-4	
B10	3856-5	
B11	3856-6	
B12	3856-7	
B16	7252	
B18	3251	
C2	1517	
C3	9117	
C5	2808†	
C6	1524	
C7	4622	
C8	3678	
C9	4627	
D1	**3668**	
D5	**2813**	
D6	3906	
D7	6504-1	
D8	**7724-1**	
D9	**7724-2**	
D10	**7724-3**	
E1	**1519**	
E2	**1518**	
E4	**1520**	
E6	**2409**	
E9	2815	
E10	4624	
E11	6860	
E12	6441	
E13	**6272**	

Table 38. Continued

Part of BS 3900	Equivalent ISO standard	Equivalent EN Standard*
F6	2810	
F8	3231	
F9	**6270**	
F12	**7253**	
F14	**11341**	
F15	11503	
G5	2812-1	
G8	2812-2	
H1	**4628-1**	
H2	**4628-2**	
H3	**4628-3**	
H4	**4628-4**	
H5	**4628-5**	
H6	**4628-6**	
J1	8130-9	
J2	8130-1	
J3	8130-6	
J4	8130-8	
J5	8130-7	
J6	8130-2	
J7	8130-3	
J8	8130-4	
J9	8130-5	

* Many of the ISO Standards listed have been issued as ENs, with related numbers (for example, ISO 1513 has been issued as EN ISO 1513, and ISO 1524 as EN 21524). These duplicated numbers are not listed in the table.

† ISO standards which are called up in EN 10169-1 and 1396 are shown in bold type.

Little stainless steel is coil coated, but EN 10088-1 covers the composition and mechanical properties of stainless steel, and pr EN 502 and 508-3 give details of appropriate alloys for roofing applications.

Powder coatings or liquid-applied coatings can be applied to the sheet and wrought products described above, but can also be applied to galvanised steel panels (of irregular shape) or to cast aluminium. These substrates continue to be covered by BS 729 and BS 1490.

4.2.3. Test methods for coatings

British Standard test methods for paints, which include chemical and physical tests on liquid paint, mechanical and durability tests on painted panels, are given in BS 3900. BSI's policy in the past was to implement new work in this field in ISO and CEN as a part of BS 3900,

Table 39. Other British Standards (CP and PD series) relevant to coated metals and related subjects

BS Number	Title	Nature of Standard	Commentary
CP3 Chapter V: Part 2	Code of basic data for the design of buildings Loading Wind loads		This remaining part of CP3 remains current, but has been superseded by BS 6399: Part 2: 1995
CP 143 Part 1: 1958 Part 3: 1964 Part 10: 1973 Part 12: 1970 Part 15: 1973	Code of Practice for sheet roof and wall coverings Aluminium, corrugated and troughed Zinc Galvanised corrugated steel Copper Aluminium	Code for profiled aluminium Profiled galvanised steel Fully supported aluminium	Standards will be withdrawn when BS 5427: Part 2 Installation is issued
PD 6484: 1979	Commentary on corrosion at bimetallic contacts and its alleviation		Considers consequences of contact between different metals

but this has changed so that now these new methods are issued as BS ISO or BS EN standards, to replace the appropriate part of BS 3900.

BS 3900 has over 100 parts which are given in Table 37 (but not itemised in full), and the relationship between BS 3900 and ISO and EN standards is given in Table 38. These methods are appropriate for all liquid paints or painted products, so can be applied to coil coatings, other liquid-applied coatings or to painted products (produced by any process). The methods in Part J are specific to powder coatings and implement ISO 8130-1 to 9 as British Standards. Work is continuing at ISO and further parts are in course of preparation.

The European Coil Coating Association has published 19 test methods for coil coatings and coil-coated products. These are being revised and publication as ECCA methods is expected early in 1997. There is current work in CEN TC 139 WG9 to adopt these methods as ENs, and seven drafts are expected to go to 'enquiry' between January and June 1997.

All the standards described in this section are test methods, so, in themselves they give no guidance to the client for coated metal roofing or cladding. The specifications described below call up these methods and either define appropriate limits of performance (or allow these to be agreed between the supplier and client) which will enable the client to use these methods effectively in the specification.

Table 40. International and European Standards implemented as British Standards, relevant to coated metals and related fields

BS Number	Title	Nature of Standard	Commentary
BS EN ISO Series			
EN ISO 1513	Paints and varnishes	Test methods	Associated with BS 3900. See Table 38
EN ISO 9000-1: 1994	Quality management and quality assurance standards: guidelines for selection and use	Quality management and assurance	Replaces BS 5750: Part 0
9001: 1994	Quality systems: model for quality assurance in design, development, production, installation and servicing		Replaces BS 5750: Part 1 Relates to ability to design and supply conforming product/ service
9002: 1994	Quality systems: model for quality assurance in production, installation and servicing		Replaces BS 5750: Part 2 Relates to ability to supply product/service to an established design
BS EN series			
EN 456, 535 and 605	Paints	Test methods	Associated with BS 3900. See Table 38
EN 485	Aluminium and aluminium alloys. Sheet, strip and plate	Requirements and tolerances for aluminium	Together EN 485,. 515 and 573 replace BS 1470
485-1: 1994	Technical conditions for inspection and delivery		
485-2: 1995	Mechanical properties		
485-3: 1994	Tolerances on shape and dimensions for hot-rolled products		
485-4: 1994	Tolerances on shape and dimensions for cold-rolled products		
EN 501: 1994	Roofing products from metal sheet. Specifications for fully supported roofing products of zinc sheet	Specification for zinc for roofing	Publication of EN 502 to 508 for roofing in other metals is expected during 1998
EN 515: 1993	Aluminium and aluminium alloys. Wrought products. Temper designations		
EN 573	Aluminium and aluminium alloys	Composition and designation of aluminium	
573-1: 1995	Numerical designation system		
573-2: 1995	Chemical symbol based designation system		

Table 40. Continued

BS Number	Title	Nature of Standard	Commentary
573-3: 1995 573-4: 1995	Chemical composition Forms of products		
EN 10088: 1995	Stainless steels		Partly replaces BS 970: Part 1
EN 10142: 1991	Specification for continuously hot-dip zinc-coated low carbon steel sheet and strip for cold forming: technical delivery conditions	Specification for galvanised steel sheet	The three standards replace BS 2989, and Euronorms 142, 143, 147 and 148
EN 10143: 1993	Continuously hot-dip metal-coated steel sheet and strip. Tolerances on dimensions and shape	Tolerances	
EN 10147: 1992	Specification for continuously hot-dip zinc-coated structural steel sheet and strip. Technical delivery conditions	Structural grades	
EN 10154	Continuously hot-dip aluminium – silicon (AS) coated steel strip and sheet. Technical delivery conditions	Specification for aluminised steel (Type 1)	Replaces BS 6536 and Euronorm 154
EN 10169-1: 1996	Continuously organic coated (coil coated) steel flat products. Part 1: General information	Specification for coil-coated steel	
EN 10204: 1991	Metallic products. Type of inspection documents	Documents for metals	
EN 10214: 1995	Continuously hot-dip zinc – aluminium (ZA) coated steel strip and sheet. Technical delivery conditions	Specification for 5% aluminium alloy coated steel	
EN 10215: 1995	Continuously hot-dip aluminium – zinc (AZ) coated steel strip and sheet. Technical delivery conditions	Specification for 55% aluminium alloy coated steel	Replaces BS 6830

4.2.4. Standards for coil-coated steel

In the past there was no British Standard for coil coatings or coil-coated products. BS 5427: 1976[30] included information on the durability of coil coatings in Appendixes D2 and E, and these data were used by the PSA (in their *Method of Building*) and the ECCS (in their guide *Good Practice in Steel Cladding and Roofing*).[10]

Table 41. *Work in progress on British and European Standards as of March 1997*

BS committee	CEN committee	Standard Number	Subject	Progress to date	Anticipated publication
ISE/10	ECISS 27	EN10169-1	Continuously organic-coated (coil-coated) steel flat products. Part 1: General information	Adopted as EN 10169-1	Published as BS EN 10169-1
		pr EN 10169-2	Part 2: Products for building exterior applications	'Enquiry' completed	February 1998
		Other parts	Other applications		
B/542		BS 5427: Part 2	Code of Practice for the use of profiled sheet for roof and wall cladding on buildings. Part 2: Installation	Not yet started	Unknown
	TC 128 SC 7	pr EN 502 503 504 505 506 507 508-1 508-2 508-3	Roofing products from metal sheet: Stainless steel* Lead* Copper* Steel* Copper or zinc† Aluminium* Steel† Aluminium† Stainless steel†	'Enquiry' completed	March 1998
	TC 128 SC 11	—	Sandwich panels	First meeting held September 1996	Pre-circulation draft expected September 1997. Completion date unknown
	TC 128 SC9/WG4	—	Fixings	Work item not yet agreed	Unknown
NFE/35	TC132	EN 1396	Aluminium and aluminium alloys — coil-coated sheet and strip for general applications. Specifications	Adopted as EN 1396	Published as BS EN 1396

*Fully supported.   †Self-supporting.

Table 41. Continued

BS committee	CEN committee	Standard Number	Subject	Progress to date	Anticipated publication
STI/10	TC 139 WG5	pr EN 12206-1	Paints and varnishes. Coating of aluminium and aluminium alloys for architectural purposes. Part 1: Coatings prepared from powder coating materials	'Enquiry' completed. Comments being considered	Unknown
		pr EN 12206-2	Part 2: Coatings prepared from liquid organic coating materials	Draft prepared still to be circulated on 'enquiry'	Unknown
	WG8		Equivalent work on powder coatings on galvanised steel	Draft prepared still to be circulated on 'enquiry'	Unknown
	WG9		Preparation of EN test methods for coil coatings, based on 19 existing ECCA methods	Seven drafts likely to be circulated on 'enquiry' between Jan–Jun 1997	Unknown
STI/10	ISO committee				
	TC 35/ SC9/WG16	ISO 8130	Testing of coating powders		
		8130-10	Determination of deposition efficiency	'Enquiry' just started	Early 1998
		8130-11	Inclined plane flow test	'Enquiry' completed	Late 1997
		8130-12	Determination of compatibility	'Enquiry' just started	Early 1998

PVC-coated steel was accepted for roofing under the Building Regulations 1976[94] and the 1985 Regulations accept PVF_2 and PVC coatings on steel and aluminium.

The first British Standard to include coil-coated steel was BS 6781, which implemented Euronorm 169 as a British Standard. Recent work in CEN has converted Euronorm 169 into EN 10169-1, which is about to be implemented as BS EN 10169-1 (when BS 6781 will be withdrawn).

EN 10169-1 is a general standard for all uses of coil-coated steel, hence it addresses some issues more relevant to industrial uses of the product and does not address external exposure in as much depth as pr EN 10169-2 (which is specifically for this use). The requirements and scope of EN 10169-1 are as follows. EN 10169-1:

(a) covers both conventional coil coatings and laminated products, and also includes powder coil-coating

      (b) draws attention to the use of strippable film to protect the coated surface but points out that the film has a limited life when exposed

      (c) includes a designation scheme which enables the characteristics of the product (including the composition of the steel, the nature and thickness of its metal coating and the nature and thickness of the organic coating on both sides) to be specified precisely

      (d) calls up a large number of ISO test methods for paints and varnishes (which are related to BS 3900 and are indicated in Table

Table 42. Equivalent guidance issued by other authoritative organisations

Organisation	Document	Scope	Comments
British Board of Agrément (BBA)	Agrément Certificates (listed in Appendix 1)	Approvals for products and systems in coated aluminium, galvanised steel, etc.	
Conseil International du Bâtiment (CIB)	Report 148. Preliminary European recommendations for sandwich panels with additional recommendations for panels with mineral wool core material	Composite panels with mineral wool core	Based on ECCS 66
Centre for Window and Cladding Technology (CWCT)	Standard for curtain walling. Guide to Good Practice for facades. Test methods for curtain walling	Considers curtain walling	Information on materials and maintenance also relevant to other forms of cladding
Department of the Environment (DOE)	Approved Document B (to Building Regulations 1991)	Design guidance on fire	Table A5 ii gives notional designation of AA for roof with profiled sheet of coil-coated steel or aluminium with PVC or PVF$_2$ coating* Table A5 v allows fully supported coil-coated steel or uncoated aluminium but appears to exclude coil-coated aluminium. Requirements B2, B3 and B4 have performance requirements (Class 0, Class 1, etc.) for internal linings, cavities and cladding, but include no equivalent deemed-to-satisfy statement†
	Approved Document C	Design guidance on water penetration	Requirement C4 refers to BS 5247, BS 8200 and CP 143, but makes no reference to BS 5427, which is also considered appropriate‡

* The same notional designations are given by the equivalent Northern Ireland Regulations. The Building Standards Scotland Regulations use the same definition, but do not state the notional designations.

† The same situation applies in Scotland and Northern Ireland.

‡ Equivalent guidance in Scotland and Northern Ireland also does not include reference to BS 5427.

Table 42. Continued

Organisation	Document	Scope	Comments
European Coil Coating Association (ECCA)	**ECCA Test Methods** T1 Coating thickness T2 Specular gloss T3 Colour difference T4 Pencil hardness T5 Resistance to rapid deformation T6 Adhesion after indentation T7 Resistance to cracking on bending T8 Resistance to salt spray fog T9 Water immersion resistance T10 Resistance to accelerated weathering using UV lamps T13 Accelerated ageing by the use of heat T14 Measurement of chalking T15 Metamerism T17 Determination of the adhesion of strippable films T18 Stain resistance T19 ECCA recommendation for panel design and method for atmospheric exposure testing T21 Method of evaluation of outdoor exposed panels T22 Visual comparison of colours T23 Colour stability in humid atmospheres containing sulphur dioxide Eurodes:	Test methods and natural exposure techniques for coil coated metals	Original methods issued 1977–1982, reviewed and revised 1996. See also CEN work under TC 139 WG9
	ECCA outdoor exposure testing facilities	Marine industrial marine high UV inland industrial sites	Natural exposure required under EN 1396 and pr EN 10169-2
	Maintenance and repairing of pre-coated metal	Maintenance procedures	
European Convention for Constructional Steelwork (ECCS)	EC20 The testing of profiled metal sheets EC40 The design of profiled sheeting EC41 Good practice in steel cladding and roofing	Agreed European recommendations for profiled sheet	Applicable to both to aluminium and steel sheeting on a steel frame
	EC62 Preliminary European recommendations for sandwich panels: Part II Good practice EC66 Part 1 Design	Agreed European recommendations for sandwich panels	See also CIB Report 148

Table 42. Continued

Organisation	Document	Scope	Comments
Metal Cladding and Roofing Manufacturers Association (MCRMA)	**Technical Design Guides** 1. Daylighting recommended good practice in metal-clad industrial buildings 2. Curved sheeting manual 3. Secret-fix roofing design guide 4. Fire and external steel-clad walls: guidance notes to the revised Building Regulations 1992 5. Metal wall cladding detailing guide 6. Profiled metal roofing design guide (revised May 1996) 7. Fire design of steel sheet clad external walls for building: Construction performance standards and design 8. Acoustic design guide for metal roof and wall cladding systems 9. Composite roof and wall cladding panel design guide 10. Profiled metal cladding for roofs and walls: guidance notes on revised building regulations 1995 parts L & F **Publications** 2. Manufacturing tolerances for profiled metal roof and wall cladding 3. Built-up metal roof and wall cladding systems, tables of insulation to achieve U values of $0.25\,\mathrm{W\,m^{-2}\,K^{-1}}$, $0.35\,\mathrm{W\,m^{-2}\,K^{-1}}$ and $0.45\,\mathrm{W\,m^{-2}\,K^{-1}}$ 6. Latent defects insurance scheme basic guide	Guidance on design of installations of profiled metal and composite panels	
National Federation of Roofing Contractors (NFRC)	**Technical Bulletins** 11. Flat metal composite wall panels — steel work tolerances 12. Seals and sealants for metal sheeting and cladding 13. Horizontal profiled metal cladding, a check list for design & workmanship 17. Rooflights **Technical Publications** Roofing and cladding in windy conditions. Profiled sheet metal roofing and cladding. 2nd edition **Guidance Notes** 5. Check list for horizontal cladding 9. Handling long profiled metal sheets	Guidance on design and installation of profiled metal and composite panels	Profiled sheet metal roofing and cladding to be revised and reissued in loose-leaf form during 1998

38): ISO 4892 Parts 1 to 4 (which are issued as BS 2782-540 D to G) and ASTM D 3363, 4145 and 4214 (which are also standard paint tests)

(e) requires the same tolerances on dimensions and shape as the standard for the steel on which the product is based

(f) defines the routine quality control tests to be conducted for coating thickness, colour, gloss, coating hardness, adhesive strength and flexibility, but only defines requirements for the tolerance on coating thickness and gloss; it requires the purchaser to define his acceptance limits for other tests (and allows other gloss limits to be set)

(g) expresses bend tests characteristics in terms of the radius of the mandrel over which the product is bent (unlike standards for uncoated metals, which use the diameter)

(h) warns that tests for colour, gloss and hardness cannot be used reliably on embossed or textured coatings (which are commonly used for external exposure)

(i) defines durability tests and external exposure procedures (by reference to the sites and procedures established by the ECCA), but does not require the durability tests to be conducted as 'part of the routine test programme following the production'

(j) requires the purchaser to give detailed information on requirements for the dimensions, documentation and marking of the product, to specify the test methods to be used and define limits on properties to be achieved

(k) gives details of storage procedures (which are considered more relevant to handling the coil than products formed from it).

pr EN 10169-2 for exterior applications of coil-coated steel (expected to be issued in February 1998) uses the definitions and designations described in EN 10169-1, but pays particular attention to the possibility of corrosive attack on the reverse side of the sheet and the consequent need for this to be coated, to the need for roofing sheets to resist damage during construction, and for the use of protective film to minimise this. In other respects, pr EN 10169-2:

(a) distinguishes between factory production control tests, initial type testing and performance tests

(b) considers the 'period of protection', until remedial action will be required to restore the corrosion protection, and suggests 5% of the surface as a criterion

(c) gives a more restricted range of coating types which are suitable for external exposure (and are considered more realistic than the wider range described in EN 10169-1)

(d) classifies the environments where the products will be in service, with linked five-point scales for type of atmosphere (i.e. location) and corrosivity and a four-point scale for exposure to UV light. These scales are defined in Table 43.

4.2.5. Standards for coil-coated aluminium

Work on coil-coated aluminium has been conducted broadly along the same lines as that on coil-coated steel, and EN 1396 has been adopted as BS EN 1396. Like EN 10169-1 for steel, EN 1396 covers coil coating with liquid coil coatings, powder coil coatings and plastic films, and embraces all uses of the coated product. There are no plans to issue a separate part of EN 1396 for external applications, but EN 1396 gives more detail on this subject than EN 10169-1.

The particular features of EN 1396 are as follows. EN 1396:

(a) calls up existing standards EN 485, 515 and 573 to define the aluminium sheet the products are based on

(b) gives an extensive list of alloys, not all of which are suitable for external exposure

(c) gives a more restricted range of coatings — apart from the 5 μm epoxy coating, all are suitable for external exposure

(d) requires coating thickness, gloss, colour and tensile tests to be conducted as routine; gives no definitive limits but makes proposals for these limits in an annex

(e) expresses bend test requirements in terms of the radius of the mandrel (like EN 10169-1)

Table 43. Classification scales defined in pr EN 10169-2

Atmosphere	A scale	Corrosivity	C scale*
Dry, internal, unpolluted	—	Very low	C1
Rural	A1	Low	C2
Urban	A2	Medium	C3
Industrial	A3	High Very high	C4 C5
Marine	A4	High Very high	C4 C5
Industrial and marine	A5	Very high	C5

UV category	Definition	
1	Reverse side of cladding or roofing	
2	N of latitude 45° N	Altitude below 900 m
3	Between latitudes of 40° and 45° N	
4	S of latitude 40° N, and any region above 900 m altitude	

*This scale has been simplified from that given in pr EN 10169-2.

Table 44. Classification scales defined in EN 1396

Category	Description	Corrosion index	UV index
1	Pre-painted metal, to receive top-coat after fabrication	—	—
2	Product for internal use	1–3	1
3	Product for external use: rural, urban tropical high UV	 2 3 2	 2 2 3
4	Product for external use: severe industrial very severe marine high UV + severe	 3 3 3	 2 2 3

(*f*) does not cover durability requirements explicitly in the standard but states 'other requirements shall be agreed by the specifier and purchaser', 'Annex C gives some guidelines', etc. (see (*g*) below)

(*g*) Annex C identifies four categories of use and three-point scales (low, medium, high) for corrosion resistance and exposure to UV light, which are explained in Table 44 (these scales thus embrace the same issues as are covered in EN 10169-1, but differ in detail).

(*h*) refers to the exposure sites established by the ECCA, and gives detailed requirements for the corrosion performance expected from panels exposed at Hendaye or the Hook of Holland and the UV performance on exposure at Lisbon or in Florida

(*i*) gives details of the corrosion performance expected from panels exposed in the salt spray test

(*j*) calls up certain ISO test methods for paints and varnishes (which are related to BS 3900, and are indicated in Table 38), ASTM D660, D3363 and G85 (which are also standard methods for paint testing)

(*k*) gives brief details of procedures for storage, forming and cleaning.

4.2.6. Standards for powder-coated products

Powder coatings and powder-coated products are already covered by British Standards 6496 and 6497, which cover the coatings, the application process, the properties of the coated aluminium and galvanised steel; require a one-year period of natural exposure in Florida; and describe the necessary precautions in transit and maintenance procedures on-site.

CEN TC 139 is developing standards with substantially the same scope and which also require a one-year natural exposure in Florida. These standards pay greater attention to the pretreatments used, include chemical and spectrometric methods to characterise the pretreatments, and require chromate-free pretreatments for aluminium to demonstrate satisfactory performance in marine and industrial conditions over two years for an interim approval and over five years for a full approval.

pr EN 12206-1 on powder-coated aluminium has completed its enquiry stage, but the equivalent drafts on powder-coated galvanised steel and liquid-applied coatings on aluminium* have still to be circulated. If these standards are adopted, they will replace BS 6496, 6497 and 4842.†

4.2.7. Standards for roofing

General
CEN TC 128's work on standards for roofing materials was supported by the European Commission through the issue of a draft provisional mandate for roofs issued in 1992. Although the character of the mandate has changed since 1992, its purpose is to generate Harmonised Standards, which address the Essential Requirements of the Construction Products Directive as well as those requirements which are normally considered in standards.

EN 501 for fully supported zinc is already in issue and considers the Essential Requirements in statements on fire, safety in use, and hygiene, health and the environment. The statement on fire refers to unfinished work in CEN TC 127, states that uncoated zinc is non-combustible, and refers to national regulations on coated zinc (pending the completion of TC 127's work). It gives a combined statement on safety in use and on hygiene, health and the environment, which does not address performance in service (as the Construction Products Directive requires) but considers questions of safety during installation (which may be the subject of other directives and national legislation, but is not considered by the CPD).

Of the drafts which have not yet been issued, pr EN 502, 505, 507 (for fully supported stainless steel, steel and aluminium) and pr EN 508-1, 2 and 3 (for self-supporting sheets of steel, aluminium and stainless steel) are relevant to this study. These drafts have completed their enquiry stages and the results of the enquiry are being considered at the time of writing.

---

*These standards cover the application of powder coatings in a conventional plant. The application of powder coatings in a coil-coating line is covered by standards for coil coating.
†These liquid-applied coatings are of no commercial significance in the UK market, but are considered in this section for convenience.

The fully supported drafts include substantially the same statement on fire as EN 501, but the statement on safety (described above) is not included. No other Essential Requirement is addressed.

The self-supporting sheet drafts include a statement on mechanical resistance, refer to the national regulations which achieve this, require the manufacturer to provide detailed information on the mechanical performance of his product*, give some calculation methods appropriate for trapezoidal sheets, and refer to the need for specific testing on other forms of the product (e.g. tiles, standing-seam systems or concealed-fix systems). The statement on fire described above is included, but there is not a statement on safety.

Note: the drafts for self-supporting sheets all refer to the national standards which are appropriate for concentrated loads, and quote 'BS 5247: Performance and loading criteria for profiled sheet in building'. These entries should be corrected and the current form of the standard should be quoted, so that the entries read 'BS 5427: The use of profiled sheet for roof and wall cladding on buildings'.

Standards for steel roofs
The statements made for coatings on each metal are the same in the standards for fully supported sheet and self-supporting sheet.

pr EN 505 and 508-1 for steel include the following.

(*a*) A range of nominal metal coating weights for the different coated steels (in their Tables 1 and 3 respectively).

(*b*) A list of the organic coatings suitable for external exposure (in their Tables 2 and 4 respectively — these coatings are tabulated in this report in Table 13 and are also included in BS 5427: 1996).

(*c*) A list of national requirements for metal coating weight (in their Table C1. This describes the Galfan ZA coating as only suitable for use in the UK with an organic coating. On present evidence this is considered justified, but it is conceivable that the heavier coating weights could perform comparably to Z350 galvanising.)

(*d*) A list of national requirements for metal coating weight for a sheet which is also to have an organic coating (in their Table C2. This describes aluminised steel with an organic coating as not permitted in the UK. There is minimal service evidence on this product, but it is considered capable of giving good service — it is recommended that the performance of this product should be investigated, and the exclusion reconsidered.)

(*e*) An Annex D, which states 'this annex will be obsolete when EN 10169-1 and 2 are issued', and effectively restates the text on

---

*A requirement which is already included in BS 5427 (1976 and 1996 editions).

coating tests from EN 10169-1, but gives details of the limits which the product must achieve. The repetition of the text of the tests is considered unnecessary, but the limits defined are considered valuable and should be retained.

(*f*) An Annex E, which also states 'this annex will be obsolete when EN 10169-1 and 2 are published'. This Annex gives a detailed review on the durability of coatings which is not included in either part of EN 10169 — this review is considered valuable and should be retained; it is reproduced as Appendix 3 to this report.

Standards for aluminium roofs
pr EN 507 and 508-2 for aluminium include:

(*a*) a range of suitable aluminium alloys in their Table 1
(*b*) a list of the organic coatings suitable for external exposure in their Table 2 (these coatings are tabulated in this report in Table 13 and are also included in BS 5427: 1996).

These drafts do not include any details of performance requirements or tests of the coatings, but include a cross reference to EN 1396.

Standards for stainless steel roofs
pr EN 502 and 508-3 for stainless steel include:

(*a*) suitable grades of stainless steel in their Table 1
(*b*) a list of organic coatings suitable for external exposure in their Table 2.

These drafts do not include any details of performance requirements or tests for the coatings, but include a cross reference to EN 10169. This cross reference is considered misleading as EN 10169 excludes stainless steel from its scope and includes no details on limits in its coating performance tests.

4.2.8. Fire

The fire properties of coated metal roofing and cladding which are controlled under the various Building Regulations in the UK are the fire roof exposure rating, and the flame spread characteristics of cladding (and its reverse side in cavity situations). The British Standards which are relevant for these properties are Parts 3, 6 and 7 of BS 476. These Standards and the Regulations which use them are still considered appropriate to control these aspects of fire performance. However, the various Regulations call up BS 476: Part 3: 1958 — which is withdrawn — and the current form of the standard, BS 476: Part 3: 1975, is not cited in the Regulations. This situation is perverse, but has been rectified to some extent by the inclusion of the text of BS 476: Part 3: 1958 as Annex E in BS 5427: 1996.

BS 476: Part 3: 1958 gives a two-letter designation which shows, first, the resistance of a roof to penetration by fire and, second, the flame spread characteristics shown by the roof in response to an external source of ignition. Conventional profiled metal sheets used in roofing are of an adequate thickness to prevent fire penetration in this test and are installed with adequate lap joints, to prevent fire penetration at the joints. Consequently products in this form need only be investigated to show their spread of flame in this test. (Other systems will need the complete test to demonstrate the response of their joints to fire conditions.) Substantial work on reaction to fire is taking place in CEN TC 127, whose aim is to produce harmonised test methods, and the European Commission are seeking to harmonise classes of performance for reaction to fire. Ultimately Regulation requirements in the UK could come to identify European classes of performance (with equivalent levels of safety to current requirements) and to refer to harmonised European methods.

4.2.9. Colour

BS 4904 defines a range of 38 preferred colours for external cladding, which are taken from a wider range of 237 colours defined in BS 5252. (BS 4800 for paint colours for buildings is also linked with BS 5252.)

BS 5252 and its related standards were created in response to an initiative from RIBA (Royal Institute of British Architects) to create a systematic colour range, to reconcile the desire of the specifier to have a realistic choice of colour with the desire of the producer to reduce the range of products which must be produced.[112] This concept is becoming of less importance for liquid paints as tinting techniques become more sophisticated, but is still important for painted products where a wide diversity of choice has implications for stock availability and cost.

BS 4904 and BS 5252 differ from other colour scales by their systematic structure. They differ from BS 381C and the RAL scale used in Germany,[113] which are both arbitrary scales, and they differ from the NCS system[114] and Munsell scales[115] which can give a designation to any colour but do not define a particular colour range.

International trade in coated metal roofing and cladding is widespread, so the consequence of the different colour scales is that manufacturers are obliged to produce a wider range of colours than is strictly necessary in order to satisfy their different markets. In effect, the existence of different national standards for colour creates a barrier to trade.

It is considered that international work to harmonise colour ranges for claddings (or possibly for painted building materials in general) is necessary. RIBA is making this initiative through British Standards committee STI/14 and ISO TC 187—it is recommended that this initiative should be supported.

4.2.10. Fixings/fasteners

Fixings for cladding and roofing are covered by BS 1494: Part 1: 1964. Stainless steel fasteners are covered by BS 6105: 1981, but this standard relates more to industrial uses than building uses of the products. BS 5427: 1996 includes a discussion on fasteners and illustrates the types that are available. In particular, it defines 'fixing' as the system connecting sheets to each other or to the structure, and 'fastener' as the main element of the 'fixing.'

Previously BS 5427: 1976 included a more detailed discussion which warned that the life of cadmium-plated fasteners was limited and referred to the use of plastic-coated fasteners and plastic heads and caps. Relevant parts of CP143 which are still current are CP 143: Part 1: 1958, Part 10: 1973 and Part 15: 1973 for aluminium profiles, galvanised steel and fully supported aluminium respectively.

Clause 2.8.3 of BS 5427: 1996 requires carbon steel fasteners (to BS 1494: Part 1) to have an adequate coating of electroplated zinc or cadmium (a statement that is difficult to reconcile with the statement in the previous standard) or to be galvanised or sherardised. It recognises that the fasteners could also have a plastic coating. It refers to aluminium fasteners (also to BS 1494: Part 1) or to stainless steel, and alerts the user to the need to avoid bimetallic corrosion (which it covers in clause 3.9).

The three parts of CP143 considered refer to BS 1494: Part 1 and to other specifications which were current when the codes were issued, but have been replaced or become out of date since. (For example, they contain references to aluminium alloys HG20 or NS6, which have been redesignated.)

There has been substantial development in the design of fasteners for cladding and roofing since 1964, which has not been adequately expressed in British Standards. There are proposals for work in CEN on this subject in TC 128, but these proposals have not been accepted to date.

As the two previous studies in this field[3,16] showed that corrosion of fasteners was a common cause of failure, it is considered imperative that there should be authoritative and widely available guidelines on the selection and use of fasteners and it is regrettable that current standards do not do this adequately.

The majority of fasteners for cladding and roofing in the UK are supplied by ITW Buildex or by SFS Stadler, both of whom are Associate Members of the MCRMA, and both of whom can supply detailed technical information on their product ranges and give technical services on design and installation. As the guidance in British Standards is inadequate, it is recommended that up to date advice on fasteners should be sought from the suppliers.

4.2.11. Rooflights

Previous studies[3,16] have reported failures associated with rooflights. There is no British Standard covering rooflights, but BS 4154 and 4230 cover corrugated sheets in GRP and PVC, which are available in the same profiles as profiled metal sheets. The mechanical properties of these sheets, their coefficients of thermal expansion and their resistance to loading are inferior to the metal roof they are used on, and single glazing using these sheets can no longer meet current insulation requirements for buildings. The sheets' inability to sustain loading has particular implications under the Construction (Design and Management) Regulations 1994,[116] as the possibility of an accident can easily be envisaged at the design stage. Consequently the use of profiled transparent plastic sheets is reducing and more sophisticated products and techniques are being developed.

The major rooflight manufacturers are Associate Members of the MCRMA who can give technical advice on their products and can provide technical service on-site. The MCRMA has published a Technical Design Guide *Daylighting — Recommended Good Practice in Metal Clad Industrial Buildings*.[13.1]

4.2.12. Design and installation

In its original form BS 5427: 1976 covered both design and installation of profiled roofing and cladding. In its present form the standard has been issued as BS 5427: Part 1: 1996 and covers design, and the design of profiled steel sheeting is also covered by another recent standard, BS 5950: Part 6: 1995.

Particular points in BS 5427: 1996 are as follows.

(a) Its inadequate treatment of the need for cooperation between different parties to the contract (which is considered in more detail in Section 4.2.13).

(b) Clause 3.13 of the current standard considers penetrations through the cladding and seeks to keep these to a minimum, to group them in such a manner that they can be made waterproof easily, and to anticipate where they may be required and make provision for them. It also requires any penetrations made after completion to be designed and constructed by competent persons. Water penetration at these details is a commonly reported source of failure[3,16] and this guidance is considered valuable.

(c) Clause 3.6 considers edge corrosion at the cut edges of steel sheeting and describes one strategy to minimise this, or the application of a paint coating to the edge.

Further work to produce BS 5427: Part 2 on installation is proposed but has yet to start, and CP 143 Parts 1 and 10 (for profiled aluminium and galvanised steel) are to be retained until this is issued. Consequently, the design of profiled sheet installations is adequately covered by recent British Standards but the information given by standards on installation can at best be considered obsolescent.

Approved Document C to the Building Regulations (England & Wales) 1991, Technical Booklet C to the Building Regulations (Northern Ireland) 1994 and deemed-to-satisfy provision G3.1v of the Building Standards (Scotland) Regulations 1990 all refer to CP 143 Parts 1 and 10, but make no reference to BS 5427. It is recommended that this situation should be reversed.

Besides BS 5427, there are other sources of authoritative information on design and installation, and their treatment of specialist systems such as composite panels and secret-fix systems is considered particularly valuable. These publications are:

(a) NHBC Guide to Good Practice, which covers both design and installation. The revision in loose-leaf form to be published early in 1997 is expected to give emphasis to installation

(b) MCRMA Design Guides on particular topics

(c) ECCS recommendations for profiled sheet on a steel structure

(d) ECCS and CIB recommendations on sandwich panels.

PSA's Method of Building publications are also considered valuable, but they do not consider recent developments.

BS 5427 and the publications described above consider profiled sheet, which is able to transmit and sustain loads. Coated sheet may also be used fully supported or may be in the form of a panel as part of a curtain wall. CP 143: Part 15: 1973 and the CWCT Guide are relevant to these techniques, and it will also be necessary for the structure they are used on to satisfy BS 6399.

4.2.13. Cooperation

BS 5427: 1976 drew particular attention in its clause 10 to the need for all parties involved in the Contract to exchange information at an early stage and in adequate detail. To some extent this standard anticipated the developments to foster cooperation which have since taken place.

Codes of Practice in other technologies, for example BS 8203: 1996 (installation of resilient floor coverings) require wide consultation between all parties involved in the project, from the design stage and throughout the contract, and seek to minimise conflicting operations in the contract through this cooperation. It is considered that this guidance is also valid for other materials and technologies.

It is regrettable that no such text is included in BS 5427: 1996 and that the guidance given in the 1976 standard on this issue is omitted.

4.2.14. Maintenance

The need for maintenance of a profiled cladding or roofing installation was considered in BS 5427: 1976. This included a detailed commentary on durability which distinguished between the ultimate life (when the protective system breaks down and ceases to protect the substrate) and the decorative life (when the appearance of the cladding and its coating is no longer acceptable). It recommended that a programme should be established to carry out inspections systematically, at least once a year, with inspections of sheeting, fixings, gutters, rainware, flashings and vapour barriers. It stated that washing with water or detergent may be necessary, and that maintenance painting could be done either to improve the appearance or to extend the life of the installation.

BS 5427: Part 1: 1996 also includes a commentary on durability and draws the same distinction between design life and decorative life. It also recommends that maintenance inspections (and the necessary remedial action) should be conducted at least once a year and gives a detailed check list of points which should be covered in the inspection. However, it differs from BS 5427: 1976 by making no reference to a systematic maintenance programme and by restricting its comments to roofs.

The need for maintenance of both roofs and walls of coated metals is considered in more detail in the ECCA recommendations *Maintenance and Repairing of Precoated Metal* and guarantees offered by manufacturers require maintenance to be conducted at least annually, or documented.

In more general terms, the economic justification for maintaining any building is considered in BS 8210: 1986. This defines the nature of the records which should be created and maintained, distinguishes between 'routine', 'general' and 'detailed' inspections, gives a check list of building elements and examples of common failures and includes a proforma for use during inspection. The instructions it gives for 'profiled metal, coated or uncoated' are 'check for corrosion at edges of sheets and signs of fixing or anchorage failures.'

Table 45. Categories for design life defined in BS 7543

Category	Description	Life	Examples
Buildings 1	Temporary	Agreed period up to 10 years	Site huts
2 3	**Short life** **Medium life**	**>10 years** **>30 years**	**Short life industrial buildings, retail and warehouse buildings** **Most industrial buildings**
4	Normal life	>60 years	New hospitals, clinics, schools colleges, etc.
5	Long life	>120 years	Civic and other prestige buildings
Components 1	Replaceable	Intended for replace-ment during life of the building	Floor coverings
2	**Maintainable**	**With proper maintenance for life of building**	**Most external claddings**
3	Lifelong	Life of building	Foundations, main structure

4.2.15. Design life

The design life of a profiled roofing or cladding is considered in BS 5427: 1996. This reproduces the guidance from the previous standard and anticipates that maintenance of components will:

(a) take place after a **short life** of **2–5 years**
(b) take place after a **medium life** of **5–10 years**
(c) take place after a **long life** of **10–20 years**
(d) not take place during the life of the building, i.e. that components have a **very long life** of **20–50 years**

The standard allows other intended maintenance or design lives to be agreed between the different parties to the work, and does not necessarily require the sheeting to have the same design life as the structure.

A broader commentary on design life is given in BS 7543: 1992. This standard is intended to stimulate serious thought by a client on his expectations from a building, hence to enable the designer to meet the client's requirements more closely. The design lives it identifies for buildings in general and components in those buildings are given in Table 45, and those parts of the Table which are relevant to this study are in bold.

During the survey reported in Chapter 1, the owners, occupiers and designers of buildings clad with coated metals were asked to describe their experience and aspirations for design life. Their replies indicated that the 'medium' and 'short' lives described in BS 7543 were broadly appropriate for their requirements, but they preferred to state these more precisely. The appendixes to BS 5427 give an indication of the design lives of the various products and these are considered realistic. It is concluded that a wide range of products is available which can meet the shorter life requirements, that the more durable products can meet a 30-year requirement without repainting, and that a planned programme of inspection, maintenance and repainting will enable a longer life to be achieved.

4.3. Conclusions

Metals

There has been substantial recent work in CEN on standards for metal sheet and coil. As a result of this work the properties, dimensions, tolerances, documentation and designations for the aluminium alloys used in coil coating are defined in EN 485, 515 and 573. Galvanised steel and requirements for coating weight are described in EN 10142, 10143 and 10147, and the equivalent information on steel with other alloy coatings is given in EN 10154, 10214 and 10215. However, all these standards cover the metal sheet as a commodity, and hence include specifications which are not appropriate for use in cladding or roofing — their value is that they enable appropriate specifications to be defined in specific standards and approvals for materials for these uses.

Powder coatings and other industrially applied coatings can be used on a wider range of metal substrates — these additional base materials can be defined by reference to various British Standards.

Coatings

Work on test methods for paint and painted products in general is taking place in ISO and CEN, and is published by British Standards as parts of BS 3900, or separately in the BS ISO and BS EN series. Many of these methods are suitable for all materials, and specific methods for powder coatings are published as parts of ISO 8130. Work is in progress on specific standards for coil coatings — until this work is complete the methods are available as ECCA test methods.

As these standards are for test methods, they include no limits on performance, but they are called up in European Standards and drafts for coil-coated and powder-coated metals, and appropriate limits of performance are defined in these standards. Until European Standards for powder-coated aluminium and galvanised steel are issued, the appropriate tests and limits are given in BS 6496-7.

Coil-coated metals

There are now European Standards for coil-coated steel (EN 10169-1) and aluminium (EN 1369). These standards relate to general uses of the coated metals (i.e. are not restricted to their use in construction). Broadly the standards for the different metals address the same issues, but there are differences in approach which show they originated in different committees where the need of the customer or specifier for a harmonised approach was not appreciated or considered.

These differences are that a second standard for external uses of coated steel is being prepared (pr EN 10169-2) — no such standard is proposed for aluminium, but EN 1396 includes more information on external exposure to compensate. EN 10169-1 gives a designation system for the coated steel which includes both the characteristics of the metal sheet and both sides of the coating, but EN 1396 has no such designation. pr EN 10169-2 and EN 1396 both give classification schemes for the environment the products are to be used in, which broadly express the same issues but define different classifications. EN 1396 includes a table of the performance expected from coated aluminium on exposure, but there is no equivalent in EN 10169.

The common features are that EN 10169-1 and EN 1396 both define the routine quality control tests to be followed. As they define few requirements and prefer to allow many properties to be set by agreement between the customer and supplier their value to the specifier of coated metal roofing and cladding is limited. However, the standard procedure and standard sites they propose for durability testing are considered valuable; specifiers are recommended to seek evidence on the external performance of any proposed specification; and suppliers are recommended to conduct this work and make it available to potential users.

Metal roofing

Work on metal roofing has also been conducted in CEN TC 128, under a draft provisional mandate/order voucher from the European Commission. Draft standards from this committee anticipate that national standards will be used in design to allow structures of profiled sheets to meet the Essential Requirements for mechanical resistance and stability, and that national standards will be used to achieve safety in fire until Harmonised Standards are available.

pr EN 505 and 508-1 (for coated steel roofing) include tables which show the range of products which are accepted for use in some countries but do not meet UK requirements, i.e. which show materials which could be supplied into the UK and used in a 'product switching' situation. Some of the restrictions on UK use may be unjustified and arbitrary, and recommendations were made in Chapter 2 for work to investigate these.

pr EN 505 and 508-1 include a detailed review on the durability of coatings which is considered valuable.

Fire

The fire requirements for coated metal roofing and cladding are defined in the various Building Regulations in terms of BS 476 Parts 3, 6 and 7. The definition uses BS 476: Part 3: 1958 (which is withdrawn) and does not use the current 1975 edition of the standard. Some order has been brought into this situation by incorporating the text of BS 476: Part 3: 1958 as an annex to BS 5427: Part 1: 1996, but it is recommended that this anomaly should be rectified more formally.

Colour

The different national colour systems create a barrier to trade and oblige manufacturers to produce and stock a wider colour range than is strictly necessary. BS 5252 and the associated standard for cladding, BS 4904, represent a systematic approach to give the specifier a realistic choice of colours across the colour range which is neither arbitrary nor diverse—RIBA's initiative to use these standards as the basis for European work is to be supported.

Fixings/fasteners and rooflights

Fixings (fasteners) and rooflights are commonly associated with failures of roofing and cladding and are inadequately covered by British Standards. The main suppliers of these products are Associate Members of the MCRMA and can give substantial guidance on the use of their products. Work is proposed on a European Standard for fixings/fasteners, and an MCRMA Technical Design Guide already covers the use of rooflights.

Design

The design of profiled sheeting installations is covered by BS 5427: Part 1: 1996 and BS 5950: Part 6: 1995. The former also gives substantial guidance on the different coatings available on metals and their durability, is in line with the current and draft European Standards for coated metals and roofing, and covers all the coated metal cladding and roofing materials in current use. It gives a particularly detailed commentary on plastisol.

BS 5427: Part 1: 1996 is considered a particularly important standard, and it is strongly recommended that designers should use it as the basis for their designs of profiled metal roofing and cladding installations. It is particularly regretted that Approved Document C to the Building Regulations 1991 and the parallel guidance in Scotland and Northern Ireland make no reference to the previous edition of BS 5427, and it is recommended that the current edition should be included at the next opportunity.

The information on the properties of the coatings given in BS 5427: Part 1: 1996 is still valid for coated metal in other forms, but the information on design is not necessarily appropriate.

Authoritative sources of design information for coated metal in other forms are the NHBC Guide, MCRMA Design Guides, ECCS publications, Agrément Certificates and the CWCT Guide, and general considerations for the structure are given in CP 3: Chapter V and BS 6399: Part 2.

Installation

The installation of profiled metal sheeting is not adequately covered by current standards, but work is proposed on BS 5427: Part 2 on installation and authoritative guidance on installation is given in the publications described above (which also cover coated metals in other forms).

Cooperation

Consultation between the different parties to a Contract, from the design stage and throughout the Contract is considered both valuable and necessary to ensure a proper understanding of the requirements of the Contract, to minimise conflicting operations and to foster prompt and effective conduct of the work. It is regrettable that BS 5427: Part 1 gives little guidance on this important issue.

Inspection and maintenance

The various standards address the need for inspection and maintenance of a coated metal installation, and manufacturers' guarantees require these to be conducted at least annually and documented. No one standard, however, addresses all the issues comprehensively. The economic justification for maintaining any building is explained in BS 8210 — it is recommended that a programme to carry out inspections and routine maintenance of a metal cladding or roofing installation should be established when or before the installation is completed, and that these should be conducted on sheeting, fixings, gutters, rainware, flashings and vapour barriers at least annually and documented.

Design life

The design lives expected by clients are broadly in line with the 'short' and 'medium' lives defined in BS 7543 — a wide range of products is capable of achieving the shorter life, the more durable products can meet a 30-year life without repainting, and a planned repainting cycle will enable a longer life to be achieved.

4.4. Recommendations

It is recommended that:

(a) current support for British participation in relevant European work should continue, in respect of:

(i) CEN TC 139 on test methods for powder coatings and coil coatings, and on standards for powder-coated aluminium and galvanised steel

(ii) ECISS 27 in progressing pr EN 10169-2 on external uses of coil-coated steel

(iii) CEN TC 128 in progressing standards for fully supported and self-supporting coated steel and aluminium roofs, and on sandwich panels

(b) British Standards Committee B/542 should make an early start and aspire to speedy completion of BS 5427: Part 2 on the installation of profiled metal roofing and cladding

(c) UK support should be given to the initiative taken by RIBA to promote the BS 5252 colour series and philosophy as a basis for a harmonised European colour range and to current initiatives in CEN TC 128 for work on fixings for cladding

(d) Specifiers of coated metal cladding and roofing seek evidence of its durability from the exposure procedures described in EN 10169 and EN 1396, and suppliers should generate this evidence and make it available

(e) Designers of profiled metal installations should use BS 5427: 1996 in their designs

(f) Approved Document C and the parallel guidance in Scotland and Northern Ireland should be amended to include reference to BS 5427: 1996

(g) Owners and occupants of coated metal installations should recognise the economic case for a planned systematic programme of inspection and maintenance

(h) Specifiers and users should require products to be covered by certification demonstrating compliance with current standards.

References

1. MOAT No 34: 1986
    Method of Assessment and Testing. Precoated metal sheet roofing and cladding.
    British Board of Agrément. October 1986.

2. Agrément Certificates.
    87/1867, 87/1869, 87/1918, 87/1964, 88/2021, 88/2125, 89/2204, 89/2267, 89/2272, 90/2509, 90/2534, 91/2574, 91/2704, 91/2705, 91/2717, 92/2815, 93/2887, 93/2918, 93/2921, 93/2922, 93/2971, 93/2973, 94/3002, 94/3028, 94/3041, 94/3046, 95/3122, 95/3161, 95/3166
    (see also Appendix 1).
    British Board of Agrément.

3. Building Research Establishment Report BR 259.
    Survey of performance of organic-coated metal roof sheeting.
    R. N. Cox, J. A. Kempster and R. Bassi.
    Building Research Establishment, December 1993.

4. BS EN ISO 9000:
    Quality management and quality assurance standards.
    BS EN ISO 9001: 1994
    Quality systems. Model for quality assurance in design, development, production, installation and servicing.
    BS EN ISO 9002: 1994
    Quality systems. Model for quality assurance in production, installation and servicing. British Standards Institution. July 1994.

5. Council Directive on the approximation of laws, regulations and administrative provisions of the Member States relating to construction products (89/106/EEC).
    European Community. December 1988.

6. Standard and Guide to Good Practice for Curtain Walling.
    Centre for Window and Cladding Technology. January 1993.

7. ECCA Test methods.
    European Coil Coating Association. 1985 to 1992.

8. EURODES.
    ECCA outdoor exposure testing facilities.
    European Coil Coating Association. 1995.

9. Maintenance and repairing of precoated metal.
    European Coil Coating Association.

10. European Recommendations for Steel Construction:
The Testing of Profiled Metal Sheets. 20 (1978).
The Design of Profiled Sheeting. 40 (1983).
Good Practice in Steel Cladding and Roofing. 41 (1983).
Mechanical Fasteners for use in Steel Sheeting and Sections. 42 (1983).
Protection against Corrosion inside Buildings. 48 (1985).
Preliminary European Recommendations for Sandwich Panels:
Part II Good Practice. 62 (1990).
Part I Design 66 (1991).
European Convention for Constructional Steelwork/Steel Construction Institute.

11. Euronorms 142, 143, 147, 148, 154, 169.
Originally published by British Standards Institution as agent for European Coal and Steel Community. Now issued as European Standards or dual-listed as British Standards.
BS EN 10142, 10143, 10147, EN 10154, BS 6536/EU 154, EN 10169 BS 6781/EU 169.
British Standards Institution.

12. Agreement on technical cooperation between ISO and CEN (Vienna Agreement).
Annex 1 to ISO Council — 1991 8.1/1.

13. Technical design guides.
1. Daylighting recommended good practice in metal clad industrial buildings.
2. Curved sheeting manual.
3. Secret fix roofing design guide.
4. Fire and external steel-clad walls; guidance notes to the revised Building Regulations 1992.
5. Metal wall cladding detailing guide.
6. Profiled metal roofing design guide (Revised May 1996).
7. Fire design of steel sheet clad external walls for building: Construction performance standards and design.
8. Acoustic design guide for metal roof and wall cladding systems.
9. Composite roof and wall cladding panel design guide.
10. Profiled metal cladding for roofs and walls: guidance notes on revised building regulations 1995 parts L & F.

Other publications.
MCRMA Membership Charter.
Manufacturing tolerances for profiled metal roof and wall cladding.
Built-up metal roof and wall cladding systems tables of insulation to achieve U values of $0.25\,\text{W}\,\text{m}^2\,\text{K}$, $0.35\,\text{W}\,\text{m}^2\,\text{K}$ and $0.45\,\text{W}\,\text{m}^2\,\text{K}$.
Latent defects insurance scheme basic guide.
Metal Cladding and Roofing Manufacturers Association 1989–96.

14. Profiled Sheet Metal Roofing and Cladding.
A guide to good practice.

2nd edition.
National Federation of Roofing Contractors Ltd. September 1991.

15. Technical Report. Sandwich panels with a CFC-free polyurethane foam core.
European Union of Agrément. July 1996.

16. Durability of cladding.
A state of the art report.
P. A. Ryan, R. P. Wolstenholme, D. M. Howell.
W. S. Atkins/Thomas Telford Services Ltd. 1994.

17. The Colorcoat Building.
The Colorcoat HP200 Guarantee.
British Steel Strip Products. November 1995.

18. Armacor Guarantee.
Versacor Guarantee.
H. H. Robertson (UK) Ltd. 1995.

19. Super Vinyl 303 plastisol.
Product guarantee: (United Kingdom and Eire).
Steelinter S.A/TAC Metal Forming.

20. BS 2989: (various editions)
Specification for continuously hot-dip zinc coated and iron-zinc alloy coated steel flat products.
British Standards Institution (various dates).

21. BS 6536: 1985
Specification for continuously hot-dip aluminium/silicon coated cold reduced carbon steel sheet and strip.
British Standards Institution. June 1985.

22. BS 1470: 1987
Specification for wrought aluminium and aluminium alloys for general engineering purposes: plate, sheet and strip.
British Standards Institution. January 1987.

23. International Designation System for wrought aluminium and wrought aluminium alloys.
The Aluminium Association. Washington DC. December 1990.

24. ISO 209: 1989
Wrought aluminium and aluminium alloys — chemical compositions and forms of products.
International Organisation for Standardisation. 1989.

25. BS 6781: 1986 EU169 — 1985
Specification for continuously organic coated steel flat products.
British Standards Institution. November 1986.

26. Stockists of Assessed Capability.
Guidance Notes on the application of BS EN ISO 9002 for Quality Management Systems in Wholesale Distribution.
BSI Quality Assurance. 1995.

27. Constructing the Team.
     Sir Michael Latham.
     Final Report of the Government/Industry Review of Procurement and
     Contractural Arrangements in the UK Construction Industry. July
     1994.

28. Training the Team.
     A Report by Working Group 6 of the Construction Industry Board.
     1996

29. BS 5427: Part 1: 1996
     Copy of Code of Practice for the use of profiled sheet for roof and wall
     cladding on buildings.
     Part 1: Design.
     British Standards Institution. July 1996.

30. BS 5427: 1976
     Code of practice for performance and loading criteria for profiled sheet
     in building.
     British Standards Institution. November 1976.

31. Method of Building MOB 01.705
     Technical Guidance.
     Sheet Cladding.
     Non loadbearing profiled asbestos cement, steel and aluminium.
     Second Edition.
     Property Services Agency. January 1979.
     This document was originally published in 1977 as Method of Building
     TP E09-200. The 1979 edition makes minor changes and introduces a
     wider range of profiles and suppliers.

32. pr EN 10169 Continuously coated (coil coated) steel flat products.
     EN 10169-1 Part 1. 1996 General information (definitions, materials
     tolerances, test methods).
     pr EN 10169-2 Part 2. Products for building exterior applications.
     British Standards Institution. 1995–6.

33. BS EN 501: 1994 to pr EN 507
     Roofing products from metal sheet.
     Specifications for fully supported roofing products of:
     EN 501 Zinc sheet
     pr EN 502 Stainless steel sheet
     pr EN 503 Lead sheet
     pr EN 504 Copper sheet
     pr EN 505 Steel sheet
     pr EN 507 Aluminium sheet.
     British Standards Institution. 1996.

34. EN 1396: 1996 Aluminium and aluminium alloys — Coil coated sheet
     and strip for general applications — Specifications.
     British Standards Institution. 1996.

35. pr EN 508 Roofing products from metal sheet — Specification for self-
     supporting products of steel, aluminium and stainless steel.
     pr EN 508-1 Part 1: Steel
     pr EN 508-2 Part 2: Aluminium

pr EN 508-3 Part 3: Stainless steel.
British Standards Institution. 1996.

36. BS 3502: Part 1: 1991 ISO 1043-1: 1987
Symbols for plastics and rubber materials.
Part 1. Schedule for symbols for plastics.
British Standards Institution. May 1991.

37. Environmental aspects of PVC.
Helle Petersen. Danish Environmental Protection Agency.
PVC New perspectives 1996. Brighton. April 1996.

38. Taking back our stolen future, Hormone disruption and PVC plastic.
Greenpeace Report. April 1996.

39. Hazardous building materials.
A guide to the selection of alternatives.
Ed. by S. R. Curwell and C. G. Marsh. March 1986.

40. A review of indoor air quality and its impact on the health and well-being of office workers.
Report EUR 14029.
P. Leinster, E. Mitchell.
Thomson Laboratories Ltd, for Directorate — General Employment, Industrial Relations and Social Affairs, Commission of the European Communities.

41. PVC and the environment.
Norsk Hydro a.s. 1992.

42. PVC in buildings.
MK Electric Ltd. 1993.

43. Pursing new horizons — taking PVC beyond the millennium.
Plenary paper J. R. Svalander. European Council of Vinyl Manufacturers.
PVC and the environment — a North American status report.
R. Burnett. The Vinyl Institute.
Ecology and economy of PVC window frames.
H. Roder. Australian Plastics Institute.
Phthalates: their effect on man and the environment in perspective.
D. F. Cadogan CEFIC.
PVC New perspectives 1996. Brighton. April 1996.

44. PVC explained.
A response to Greenpeace UK's anti-pvc campaign.
British Plastics Federation. June 1996.

45. Toxicity review 14.
Review of the toxicity of the esters of o-phthalic acid (phthalate esters).
K. N. Woodward, A. M. Smith, S. P. Mariscotti, N. J. Tomlinson.
Health and Safety Executive. January 1986.

46. Chemicals and reproductive health.
Toxic Substances Bulletin. Issue 29.
Health and Safety Executive. January 1996.

47. Environmental impact of materials.
Special Publication 116.
CIRIA 1995.

48. The Green construction handbook.
A manual for clients and construction professionals.
J. T. Design Build Ltd. 1993.

49. How my work triggered the milk fiasco.
Dr Richard Sharpe, Reproductive Biology Unit, Medical Research Council.
Daily Telegraph, 5th June 1996.

50. Do man-made chemicals endanger fertility?
Working paper.
European Science and Environmental Forum. June 1996.

51. Agrément Certificate 95/3161 Detail Sheet 3.
Becker Industrial Coatings Ltd.
Becker Coil Coatings.
Beckrytech 5000.
British Board of Agrément. July 1995.

52. Dobel PVC foodsafe film laminate.
Technical data sheet ref. CL24.
Dobel Coated Steel Ltd. July 1990.

53. Controllac 180 series.
Scotchcal 100/100F and 220 series.
3M United Kingdom PLC.

54. Private communication.
3M United Kingdom PLC.

55. Survey reply.
Wardle Storeys. July 1995.

56. BS 8200: 1985
Code of practice for design of non-loadbearing external vertical enclosures of buidings.
British Standards Institution. 1985.

57. Survey reply.
Courtaulds Nippon Paint. October 1995.

58. The Robertson Cladding Manual.
H. H. Robertson (UK) Ltd. February 1995.

59. Agrément Certificates 82/989, 82/990 and 83/1098.
H. H. Robertson UK Ltd.
Versacor A, Novaclad and Versacor DF.
British Board of Agrément 1982–3.

60. BS 6496: 1984
Specifcation for powder organic coatings for application and stoving to aluminium alloy extrusions, sheet and preformed sections for external architectural purposes, and for the finish on aluminium alloy, extrusions, sheet and preformed sections coated with powder organic

coatings.
British Standards Institution. 1984.

61. BS 6497: 1984
Specification for powder organic coatings for application and stoving to hot-dip galvanized hot-rolled steel sections and preformed steel sheet for windows and associated external architectural purposes, and for the finish on galvanised steel sections and preformed sheet coated with powder organic coatings.
British Standards Institution. 1984.

62. pr EN 12206-1
Paints and varnishes — Coating of aluminium and aluminium alloys for architectural purposes.
Part 1: Coatings prepared from powder coating materials.
British Standards Institution. 1996.

63. Advances in powder coating technology for automotive applications.
G. Bell. Courtaulds Coatings Ltd.
Interfinish 96 World Congress. Birmingham. September 1996.

64. Interpon D525.
RIBA product data, product data sheet and brochure.
Courtaulds Coatings Ltd. 1993–4.

65. Interpon D 94 Gloss.
Interpon D 94 Matt.
Product data sheet.
Courtaulds Coatings.

66. Continuous powder coating lines for steel strip.
Brochure.
SMS Schloemann — Siemag AG. 1996.

67. Secretary of State's Guidance.
Powder Coating Processes, including Sherardizing.
Environmental Protection Act 1990, Part 1.
Department of the Environment. PG 6/31(96). May 1996.

68. PVDF powder coatings.
B. van de Meiyden, Sigma Coatings BV.
Thermoset Powder Coatings.
FMJ International Publications. June 1989.

69. Agrément Certificate 88/2021
PPG Industries (UK) Ltd.
Duranar and Duranar XL.
British Board of Agrément. March 1988.

70. Agrément Certificate 92/2831
Croda Mebon Ltd.
Megaflon.
British Board of Agrément. September 1992.

71. The present status of zinc-nickel alloy coatings.
S. A. Watson. Nickel Development Inst. Toronto.
Interfinish 96 World Congress. Birmingham. September 1996.

72. EH 40/xx Occupational exposure limits 19xx
     Health and Safety Executive. April 19xx (annual publication)

73. Toxicity Review 21.
     The toxicity of chromium and inorganic chromium compounds.
     S. Fairhurst and C. A. Minty.
     Health and Safety Executive. 1989.

74. Occupational Exposure Limits:
     Critical document summaries.
     Health and Safety Executive 1992.

75. Control of Substances Hazardous to Health Regulations 1988.
     Approved Codes of Practice.
     Control of substances hazardous to health.
     Control of carcinogenic substances.
     Health and Safety Commission. 1988.

76. Control of Substances Hazardous to Health Regulations 1994.
     Approved Codes of Practice.
     Control of substances hazardous to health.
     Control of carcinogenic substances.
     Health and Safety Commission. 1995.

77. Drinking Water Quality.
     Water Services Association. 1992.

78. Product data sheet.
     Novacoat 545.
     Novamax Technologies Ltd.

79. Chromium free pretreatments prior to painting.
     K. Brown. Brent Europe Ltd.
     Interfinish 96 World Congress. Birmingham. September 1996.

80. The UK Environment.
     Department of the Environment. 1992.

81. Secretary of State's Guidance.
     Coil coating processes.
     Environmental Protection Act 1990, Part 1.
     Department of the Environment PG 6/13(91) July 1991 and PG
     6/13(97) March 1997.

82. Annual Review 1995.
     Paint Research Association.

83. Private correspondence.
     Air Quality Division.
     Department of the Environment. December 1995.

84. Product information.
     Coilon Touch up EG-212.
     Becker Industrial Paint Division. February 1982.

85. The Colorcoat Building.
     Inspection and maintenance.

Appendix: Maintenance.
British Steel Strip Products. February 1996.

86. Technical brochure.
Steelseal 3.
Nobel Coatings Ltd.

87. Technical brochure.
U-coat panel coating system.
Metrotect Specialist Coatings Ltd.

88. Technical brochure.
Seamsil.
Delvemade Ltd.

89. Technical brochure.
Triskell steel.
Chemplas Triskell.

90. Agrément Certificate 93/2974.
David Roofing.
The Rubersil spray-applied Urethane foam roof insulation (and silicone rubber weather protection).
British Board of Agrément. December 1993.

91. Good roofing and cladding.
Guides 1–4.
Engineered Panels in Construction.

92. An investigation of insulated cladding constructions for industrial buildings.
P. J. Jones and G. Powell.
Welsh School of Architecture.
University of Wales College of Cardiff. August 1993.

93. The Science and Technology of Traditional and Modern Roofing Systems.
Volume One. Roofing.
H. O. Laaly. 1991.

94. Butler MR 24 Roofing system.
Technical Booklet. November 1989.

95. Roofing and Cladding.
Hoogovens Aluminium Building Systems. January 1996.

96. Brochures.
Alucobond Ecoclad and Alucore.
Alusingen GmbH.

97. Brodclad Pre-bonded Cladding systems.
Broderick Structures Ltd. January 1994.

98. Fulmer Materials Optimiser.
Volume 2 Section D Aluminium and its alloys.
Ed. N. A. Waterman.
Osco Ltd. 1974.

99.   The Building Regulations 1976.
      Statutory Instrument 1976 No. 1676.
      HMSO.

100. Colorcoat Hyclad.
      British Steel Strip Products. November 1995.

101. The performance levels of some commercial coil-coating materials.
      H. J. Tiemens and M. Hoeflaak.
      Construction and Building Materials 1994, Volume 8, No. 4.

102. Galvalume: Its prepainted corrosion performance and application in Japan.
      J. Oka.
      ECCA November 1990 Congr-Conf transcripts.

103. Materials defects highlighted by metal roof study.
      T. Bohlerengen.
      Construction and Building Materials Vol 3, No. 1 March 1989.

104. Roofing Fasteners: Field study 1985 of roofs with mechanically attached bituminous or polymeric membranes.
      Recommended corrosion protection of metallic fasteners.
      E. M. Paulsen.
      NBI Research Report No. 21 1987.

105. 1995 Product Capability Directory.
      National Coil Coaters Association. 1995.

106. The influence of Marine Environments on Metals and Fabricated Coated Metal Products, Freely Exposed and Partially Sheltered.
      G. A. King and D. J. O'Brien.
      Atmospheric Corrosion, ASTM STP 1239, 1994.

107. The influence of marine environments on the relative corrosion performance of zinc and the zinc-based alloys used for steel sheet applications.
      G. A. King.
      4th International Zinc Coated Sheet Conference. 1994.

108. Guidelines for the technical assessment of coil-coated product. 1983.
      I. D. MacGregor.
      BRANZ Technical Paper P 38.

109. Maintenance coating of painted steel structures.
      BRANZ Building Information Bulletin 253 (1987).

110. Avoiding corrosion problems in buildings.
      BRANZ Information Bulletin 254 (1987).

111. Claddings in corrosive environments.
      BRANZ Information Bulletin 332 (1995).

112. Architects' attitudes to the British building colour standards and colour use in buildings.
      T. W. A. Whitfield, M. O'Connor and T. J. Wiltshire.
      Die Farbe 32/33 (1985/86).

113. RAL colour presentation programme.
      RAL German Institute for Quality Assurance and Labelling.

114. Natural Colour System.
      Swedish Standards Institute and Scandinavian Colour Institute. 1986.

115. Standard Method of specifying colour by the Munsell system.
      ASTM D 1535.
      American Society for Testing and Materials.

116. Construction (Design and Management) Regulations 1994.
      HMSO. 1994.

Detailed references to relevant standards and other authoritative documents are given in Tables 10,11,12, 20, 37, 40 and 42.

A list of relevant Agrément Certificates is given in Appendix 1.

The references given in these tables and the Appendix are not necessarily repeated in the above list of references.

Appendices

APPENDIX 1

Current Agrément Certificates for coated metals

Certificate number	Holder	Product
Structural roofing systems		
87/1867	Stramit	Speeddeck
88/2125	Hoogovens	Kal-Zip
89/2204	British Alcan	Rigidal Super Lokroll
90/2534	Butler Building	MR-24
92/2815	TAC Metal Forming	Tacdeck 508
94/3002	Talfab	Talfab Profiles
94/3046	European Profiles	Clipfix 750
Pressed metal tiles		
87/1918	Rannilla Steel	Rannilla PVF_2 tilesheets
89/2267	Tufftile	Tufftile
89/2272	Tileform	Tileform
90/2509	Link Build	Terraplegel
91/2574	Stramit	Stramtile
95/3122	Decra	Decra Roofing System
Coated aluminium coil		
87/1964	Reynolds	Reynolux Polyester
		Reynolux PVF_2
		Reynolux PRA
93/2887	Firsteel	Firsteel Polyester
		Firsteel Polyurethane (PRA)
		Firsteel PVF_2
93/2918	Hydro Aluminium	Hydrocoat Polyester 100
		Hydrocoat PVF_2 300
		Hydrocoat Textured 800 (PRA)
93/2922	Alumax	Alumax Polyester
		Alumax PVF_2
		Alumax ARS (PRA)
Coated steel coil		
91/2717	British Steel	Architectural Polyester
		Silicone Polyester
		HP200 (Plastisol)
		Colorcoat PVF_2
		Colorcoat Hyclad
93/2921	Euramax/Alumax	EX 200 Plastisol

Continued

Certificate number	Holder	Product
93/2973	Dobel	Euromax PVF$_2$ 200 XT Plastisol Dobel PVF$_2$ External Polyester Lining Enamel Foodsafe Laminate Plastisol shot-blast
95/3166	TAC Metal Forming	Estetic Plastisol
Powder coating 91/2704 91/2705 94/3028 94/3041	International Leavlite Herberts Syntha Pulvin	Interpon D Leavlite Polyester Spectrum 2 Syntha Pulvin/Synthatec
Other coatings (for industrial applications to metal) 88/2021 95/3161	PPG Becker	Duranar Coil Coatings
Aluminium–zinc alloy coatings 87/1869 93/2971	British Steel Dobel	Zalutite Aluzinc

APPENDIX 2

Summary of replies to postal surveys, from manufacture to construction

Page	Subject	Number of surveys sent	Number returned
156	Coil coatings	10	5
157	Pretreatment	5	3
158	Coil coaters	12	8
159	Industrially applied coatings	24	8
160	Powder coatings	9	4
—	Steel coil	2	0
—	Aluminium coil	1	0
161	Roll formers	16	9
162	Polymer manufacturers	3	2
163	Film for laminates	5	2
—	Laminate producers	2	0
164	Adhesives	12	4
165	Specifiers	679*	42
167	Installers	679*	22
169	Occupiers	679*	11
170	International survey	28	10
175	Miscellaneous	7	11†

*These surveys were sent to companies known to have some experience of the product. The exact nature of this experience was not always clear in advance, and the surveys were intended to cover all three possibilities. The relatively low level of response to these surveys should be noted; it is thought that contacts would be more likely to respond if they had experienced problems with the products and so it is assumed that the remaining contacts have no adverse comments to offer.

†Includes replies to other surveys found difficult to categorise. A total of three forms were returned by the postal services, since the companies concerned were no longer trading at their last known addresses. In some cases returned forms contained no useful information; these replies are excluded from the summaries given below.

Survey of coil coating manufacturers (five replies)

Question	Summary
1. What types of coil coatings do you manufacture?	Polyester (5 replies), plastisol (4), abrasion-resistant system (4), PVF_2–acrylic 70:30 (4), PVF_2–acrylic 85:15 (1), organosol (2), silicone–polyester (2), alkyd (2), acrylic (1), high-build polyurethane (1) and vinyl (1).
2. What ancillary materials do you produce?	Primers for aluminium (5), galvanised steel (5), aluminium–zinc alloy (2), crs (1) and stainless (1). Backing lacquers (5) and paints (3), protective clear coats (3) and touch-up paints (3).
3. Are any of the products available as metallics?	All contacts manufacture metallic coatings, but two gave no details. The remaining three offer the following types: polyester (3), PVF_2 (3), alkyd (1), plastisol (1), abrasion-resistant system (1) and polyurethane (1).
4. Are any of the products formulated on latex systems?	No in three cases. The remaining two contacts did produce such systems, but gave no details.
5. Are any of the range for direct application to metals?	Two contacts manufactured polyesters that could be directly applied to metals, but one expressed doubts as to whether this would actually be done.
6. Are there other materials in development?	Yes in three cases, but little detail given. 'Superdurable' polyesters mentioned in one reply.
7. Are there other materials in your range intended for other applications, but that have potential for the construction industry?	Two replies mentioned alternative pretreatment systems derived from the automotive industry. Other possibilities included polyurethanes (in two replies), high-gloss polyesters and different backing coats.
8. Does your product range include products which are applied by another industrial process?	No in three cases. One contact manufactures an industrially applied PVF_2 system and touch-up paints. The remaining reply stated that such coatings were available but gave no details.
9. What release testing/process controls do you operate?	One contact gave no details. The remaining replies described the testing they carry out on each produced batch. This was found to vary between companies and product, but appears to be comprehensive.
10. What reference testing do you conduct on materials after they are released?	None normally undertaken other than weathering trials. Two companies reported that samples are retained for later testing if required.
11. Is your production covered under the ISO 9000 series?	Yes in four cases. The remaining contact had applied for registration, but had yet to complete the process.
12. What support do you offer your customers on problems in their production?	Two companies have specialised Technical Service Departments. The other three offer advice from their technical personnel where required.
13. What support do you offer regarding problems in service?	All contacts offer site visits and technical back up.
14. What equipment do you have available for product testing?	One contact gave no details. The equipment used by the others was listed and in every case included mechanical testing (such as impact and bend) and corrosion cabinets (salt spray, prohesion, SO_2, QUV, etc.).
15. What facilities do you have for external exposure testing?	All contacts use exposure sites, summarised geographically as follows: UK (5), Florida (5), Arizona (3), Scandinavia (2), France (1), Holland (1) and Portugal (1).

Survey of pretreatment manufacturers (three replies)

Question	Summary
1. What products do you offer for coil coating lines on:	
a) galvanised steel?	Various treatments, described by the manufacturers as follows: cleaners (6 products), conversion coatings (3), passivation rinses (2), dry-in-place treatments (2), conditioner (1), chromates (1), phosphates (1), inhibitor (1), oxidation, reacting and passivating rinses (1) and adhesion enhancer/corrosion inhibitor (single product) (1). Applied by spray, dip, roller coater, chemical coater and reaction cell.
b) aluminium–zinc alloy coated steel?	Cleaners (6), passivation rinses (3), dry-in-place treatments (3), chromate (1), conversion coatings (2) and adhesion enhancer/corrosion inhibitor (1). Applied by spray, dip, chemical coater and reaction cell.
c) aluminium?	Cleaners (2), passivation rinses (3), dry in place treatments (2), chromate (2), conversion coatings (2) and adhesion enhancer/corrosion inhibitor (1). Applied by spray, dip, chemical coater and reaction cell.
d) stainless steel?	Cleaners (2), dry in place treatment (1), chromate (1) and adhesion enhancer/corrosion inhibitor (1). Applied by spray, dip and chemical coater.
2. What products do you offer for powder coating lines on:	
a) galvanised steel?	Passivating rinses (5), conversion coatings (5), cleaners (3), refining agent (1), chromate (1) and phosphate (1). Applied by spray and dip.
b) aluminium–zinc alloy coated steel?	Passivating rinses (5), conversion coatings (4), cleaners (3), refining agent (1), chromate (1) and phosphate (1). Applied by spray and dip.
c) bare steel?	Passivating rinse (5), cleaner coaters (3), cleaners (2), conversion coatings (2), refining agent (1), phosphate (1) and conditioner (1) Applied by spray and dip.
d) aluminium?	Conversion coatings (5), passivating rinses (4), cleaners (3) etch cleaners (2), chromates (2), etching agent (1), desmut (1), refining agent (1) and deoxidiser (1). Applied by spray and dip.
e) stainless steel?	Cleaners (2), passivating rinses (2), etching agent (1), cleaner coater (1) and dry-in-place system (1). Applied by spray, dip and chemical coater.
3. Do you have other products in development for these purposes?	Yes in all cases. Developments are aimed at chromate-free products, and other health and safety/waste disposal improvements.
4. What release testing and controls do you operate?	All products are subject to quality control testing, but specific details were not given.
5. Is the process covered under the ISO 9000 series?	Yes in all cases.
6. What support do you offer to coating companies on problems in production?	Factory visits and laboratory back up. At least one company carries out routine performance testing of the coated products.
7. What support do you offer regarding problems in service?	All three companies offer technical support and laboratory testing.

Survey of coil coaters (seven usable replies)

Question	Summary
1. What substrates do you coat?	Galvanised steel (6 replies), aluminium (5), aluminium–zinc alloy coated steel (3), stainless steel (1) and steel (1).
2. What is your pretreatment sequence?	Various processes described, all of which included cleaning, degreasing and rinsing. Other features described included chromate (5) (including one no rinse), passivation (2) and mechanical abrasion (1).
3. What are the line dimensions and speed?	The line dimensions varied between coaters with the minimum width being 300 mm and the maximum 1650 mm. Quoted line speeds were 30 m/min (1), 40 m/min (1), 60 m/min (3) and 120 m/min (1).
4. Which top-coats do you use?	Polyester (7), PVF_2 (7), plastisol (5), abrasion resistant system (5), silicone–polyester (4), acrylic (2), polyurethane (1), laminate (1) and organosol (1). The following products are available as metallics from at least one supplier: PVF_2, plastisol, acrylic, abrasion-resistant system and polyester.
5. What backing coats do you use?	Polyester (6), epoxy (4), epoxy/phenolic (2), plastisol (2), organosol (1), PVF_2 (1) and alkyd (1). A common alternative is to use the same finish as the face side.
6. For what uses are your product intended?	Roofing (7), cladding (7), caravans (3), rainwater products (2), transport (2), cabins (1), white goods (1) and signs (1).
7. What quantities are used each year?	The figure given varied widely. It is not possible to draw any firm conclusions from these data due to the number of possible combinations of substrate/coating/application.
8. Are there other products in your range that could be used in building?	One contact suggested that structural roofing and cladding trays could replace purlins and rafters. No other products were mentioned.
9. What in-line controls do you operate?	Differing degrees of detail given by the individual contacts — where specified the controls include pretreatment checks, visual examination of the coil, mechanical tests (such as adhesion) and checks on curing oven temperatures.
10. What final testing do you carry out on the coil?	Again the details given varied between companies — typical tests include colour, flexibility, impact, solvent resistance and thickness.
11. Is the process covered under the ISO 9000 series?	Yes in six cases, with the remaining contact having made an application for registration, but not yet having completed the process.
12. Do you roll form the material yourselves?	Three contacts did not roll form, but supplied coil to other companies for processing. Two respondents rolled formed their own product and a single company both roll formed and supplied coil to others. One contact did not respond to this question.
13. Are you aware of any problems encountered in service?	Two companies had experienced problems with cut edges, said to be the result of poor maintenance. These had been resolved by remedial work and recoating. The remaining five companies reported no problems.

One further reply was received, but this contact produced material solely for packaging, and so could offer no information relevant to this work.

Survey of industrially applied coating manufacturers (four usable replies)

Question	Summary
1. What types of coatings do you produce for this application?	One company stated 'all types — one pack, two pack, air drying, stoving, etc'. Individual coating types identified by the other surveys comprised alkyd (2 replies), polyurethane (2), polyester (1), PVF_2 (1) and epoxy primers (1).
2. For what substrates do you recommend them?	Galvanised steel (4), aluminium–zinc alloy coated steel (4), aluminium (3), steel (3) and plastics (2).
3. Are any available in *a*) metallics? *b*) a textured finish? *c*) different gloss levels?	Yes in all four cases. Yes in all four cases. Yes in all four cases.
4. How are they applied?	Spray (4), brush (3), coil (2), roller (1), dip (1) and electrostatic (1).
5. Do you have any relevant materials in development?	One company was working towards water-based polyurethanes, one had development materials but gave no details and the remaining two contacts had no relevant materials to discuss.
6. What process controls do you operate?	Two companies described the quality controls operated, but gave little detail and the remaining two contacts supplied no information.
7. What controls do you operate on the final product?	All four companies confirmed that routine quality control tests were carried out but gave few details as to the methods used.
8. Is the process covered under the ISO 9000 series?	Yes in all four cases.
9. Do you operate an approved applicator scheme?	Yes in three cases, although for one contact this applied to only some of their product range.
10. If so, describe the controls exercised.	Two companies offered help with the initial set up and training. Three operate a system of regular visits to their approved applicators and at least one combined this with the routine testing of sample panels.
11. What support do you offer on problems with clients' production?	All four companies offered technical service visits and advice on the appropriate remedial action.
12. What support do you offer on problems in service?	In every case, site visits and sample analysis were available.
13. What test equipment do you have available?	The equipment described varied between each contact, but can be divided into mechanical testing (such as impact and extensibility) and corrosion cycling cabinets (QUV, salt spray, etc.)
14. What facilities do you use for external exposure testing?	UK (4), Florida (3), Arizona (2), France (1) and Scandinavia (1).

In addition, one reply was received from a company that manufactured air stoved coatings for application both in factories and on-site, but no details were given. Three other forms were returned indicating that the companies concerned did produce industrially applied coatings, but that these materials were intended for use on cladding or roofing.

Survey of powder coating manufacturers (three usable replies)

Question	Summary
1. What types of powder coatings do you produce for this application?	Polyester (3 replies), including 'superdurables' and thermo-plastic (1).
2. For what substrates do you recommend them?	Aluminium (3), galvanised steel (2), aluminium–zinc alloy coated steel (1), uncoated steel (1) and zinc sprayed steel (1).
3. Are any available in (a) metallics? (b) a textured finish? (c) different gloss levels?	Yes in one case, no in the remaining two (although one of these has a 'similar' product available) Yes in one case, no in the remaining two Yes in all three cases.
4. Do you have any relevant materials in development?	One company stated that they operate a continuous process of development towards more durable resins. The other two reported no developments.
5. What process controls do you operate?	All three companies conduct tests on the raw materials, and on the pre-mix, extrusion and milling stage.
6. What control do you exercise over the final product?	Powder and sample panels are tested, but it was noted that any problems are difficult to rectify when the process is complete (hence the in-process testing described above).
7. Is the process covered under the ISO 9000 series?	Yes in all three cases.
8. Do you operate an approved applicator scheme?	Yes in two cases (although only for certain products for one of the contacts). The remaining contact does not operate such a scheme.
9. If so, describe the controls exercised.	Both companies conduct regular visits and test applicators' sample panels.
10. What support do you offer on problems with clients' production?	In every case, technical service visits are carried out and facilities are available for analysis and testing.
11. What support do you offer on problems in service?	As above.
12. What test equipment do you have available?	All three contacts described both mechanical test equipment (such as bend, impact, etc.) and cyclic corrosion cabinets (QUV, salt spray, etc.).
13. What facilities do you use for external exposure testing?	Florida (3), UK (2) and Arizona (1).

A further reply was recived stating that the manufacturer did not produce materials for this application

Survey of roll formers (nine replies)

Question	Summary
1. What metals do you use?	Aluminium (8 replies), galvanised steel (8), steel (1), aluminium – zinc alloy coated steel (1), copper (1) and stainless steel (1).
2. What coatings?	PVF_2 (9), plastisol (8), polyester (7), polyamide (2), polyurethane (2), lining enamel (2), epoxy (1), silicone – polyester (1) and unspecified other (1).
3. What profiles do you form?	Full details supplied.
4. Do you have other relevant pressed products?	Secret-fix systems (5), composite panels (4), standing seam (2), flashings (2), gutters (1), acoustic systems (1), fire systems (1) and zeds, etc. (1).
5. How is the sheet protected for delivery to site?	Various combinations described in the surveys, typically including protective scrap sheets/timber bearers and banding. Strippable film used with PVF_2.
6. Do you supply any uncoated material for cladding or roofing?	Eight of the nine supplied uncoated products, broken down as follows: galvanised steel (4), aluminium (unspecified finish) (3), milled aluminium (2), stucco embossed aluminium (1), aluminium – zinc alloy coated steel (1), copper (1) and stainless steel (mill finish) (1).
7. Describe your quality control arrangements	Different degrees of detail given in the replies — generally in accordance with the companies' ISO 9000 procedures.
8. Is the process covered under the ISO 9000 series?	Yes in all nine cases.
9. What support do you offer on problems in service?	At least eight offered site visits, four of which stated that these would be in combination with the raw material supplier where appropriate. Installer training was mentioned in one case and a single contact offered long-term guarantees.

Survey of polymer manufacturers (two replies)

Question	Summary
1. What products do you offer for use in coil coatings?	PVF_2 (both replies) and polyamides (1).
2. What products do you offer for use in other relevant coatings?	Polyamides and primers for powder coating applications.
3. Do you have products under development for	
(a) technical improvements?	Auto adherent powder coatings (1) and increased gloss range for PVF_2 (1).
(b) greater ease of use?	More tolerant powder coatings (1) and room-temperature curing PVF_2 (1).
(c) health and safety benefits?	Higher solids content (2) and water-based products (1).
(d) environmental improvements?	As (c)
4. What process controls or release testing do you operate?	Details were provided of the tests carried out; these varied slightly but both included melt viscosity, particle size and colour checking.
5. Is the process controlled under the ISO 9000 series?	Yes in both cases.
6. What support do you offer on problems with customers' production?	Both contacts have customer service departments.
7. What support do you offer on problems in service?	One contact offers laboratory testing of coated products. The other survey gave no information.
8. What test equipment do you have available?	One company has comprehensive cyclic corrosion cabinets and mechanical test apparatus. The other has limited artificial weathering apparatus and external exposure facilities.
9. What facilities do you use for external exposure testing?	Florida (2) and Arizona (1).

Survey of laminate film manufacturers (two replies)

Question	Summary
1. What products do you offer for use as film laminates?	PVC (four products).
2. Do you have products under development for	
(a) technical improvements?	One company stated an ongoing aim to improve ageing.
(b) greater ease of use?	One contact was working on improving ease of application.
(c) health and safety benefits?	No.
(d) environmental improvements?	The contacts had either already removed cadmium from the formulations or were working towards this aim.
3. What process controls or release testing do you operate?	The details given varied but included thickness, colour, elongation etc.
4. Is the process controlled under the ISO 9000 series?	Yes in both cases.
5. What support do you offer to laminating companies on problems with production?	Service personnel are available for training and on problems related either to materials or application.
6. What support do you offer on problems in service?	Technical service personnel and laboratory back up.
7. What test equipment do you have available?	Full details were supplied — equipment available included mini laminator, QUV, salt spray, xenon arc, etc.
8. What facilities do you use for external exposure testing?	One company used ECCA sites. The other had a world-wide selection, including Europe, Japan, Australia and America.

Survey of adhesive manufacturers (four replies)

Question	Summary
1. What adhesives do you offer for use in composite panels?	Polyurethanes (six products), vinyl oxiranes (3), acrylics (3) and SBR (1). One contact did not manufacture such products.
2. What adhesives do you offer for use in laminating plastic films to metals?	Polyurethane (1) and polyester (1). Two contacts did not offer these materials.
3. Do you have products under development for	
(a) technical improvements?	Improved curing (1), new substrates (1) and increased fire performance (1).
(b) greater ease of use?	New spray equipment (1).
(c) health and safety benefits?	Solvent removal (2) and recyclable containers (1).
(d) environmental improvements?	Removal of solvent (2) as above.
4. What process controls or release testing do you operate?	All four surveys stated that their controls were operated in accordance with their ISO 9000 procedures (no details given).
5. Is the process controlled under the ISO 9000 series?	Yes in three cases. The fourth contact has the procedures in place, but has yet to complete the registration process.
6. What support do you offer on problems with customers' production?	Technical support is available in all four cases. The amount of detail given varied between surveys — two companies reported that visits are made, with testing as required in one case. No other information was supplied.
7. What support do you offer on problems in service?	As question 6 above.
8. Do you supply other materials that could be used for the installation of cladding or roofing panels?	No in two cases. The other two companies supply various sealants (7), fixing adhesive (1) and corrosion protection coatings (1).

Survey of specifiers (thirty-seven usable replies)

Question	Summary
1. What products have you used?	
(a) substrate	Galvanised steel (34 replies), aluminium (24), aluminium coated steel (7), aluminium–zinc alloy coated steel (6), low carbon steel (1) and aluminium with zinc protective coating (1).
(b) coating	Plastisol (29), polyester (17), PVF$_2$ (18), unspecified powder coating (10), acrylic (4), enamel (2), acrylic (1), alkyd (1), abrasion resistant system (1) and vinyl copolymer (1).
(c) process	Powder coated (24), coil coated/roll formed (22), pressed tiles (5) and spray (1). Two replies gave no details.
2. How long have you been using the products in question?	<1 year (1), 1–5 years (5), 6–10 years (7), 10–15 years (10), 16–20 years (6) and >20 years (8).
3. What time period do you expect	
(a) until repainting?	<5 years (1), 5–10 years (1), 10–15 years (6), 16–20 years (10), 21–25 years (5) and >25 years (3). Six replies did not give a figure, and a further five felt that the product would not require overcoating.
(b) until sheet replacement?	<20 years (1), 20–30 years (11), 31–40 years (7), 41–50 years (6) and >50 years (4). The remaining eight replies gave no time period.
4. Indicate the supplier of each material*	UK (65 mentions), Germany (4), Scandinavia (2), Sweden (4), Switzerland (2), Belgium (2), Austria (1), Eire (1) and South Africa (1). One reply stated that the product was imported, with no further details.
5. For what purpose?	Cladding (33), roofing (32), internal lining (14), in-fill panels (11), curtain walling (10), fascias (1), soffits (1), windows (1), gutters (1), balustrades (1) and railings (1). Constructions used (where stated): composite panels (23), single skin (14) and insulation/liner trays (11).
6. What types of buildings?	Commercial (21), industrial (19), residential (10), leisure (7), educational (6), train station (1) and tunnel lining (1).
7. In what environments?	Urban (26), rural (15), industrial (14) and coastal (8). Four replies gave no information.
8. Are you aware of any problems encountered with installation?	None (17), workmanship (7), damage to sheets (3) colour variation (2), low coating thickness (1), coating delamination (2), fixings leaking (1) and colour fading of fixings (1). Four replies failed to respond to this question.
9. Was any action taken to protect cut edges?	None (18), yes (7), yes, in certain situations only (3). One assumed protected and one stated that it was not necessary, since coated after cutting. One comment that the treatment used (zinc rich paint) was poor. The remaining seven replies made no comment.

Continued

Question	Summary
10. Have you experienced any problems in service?	None (12), cut edge corrosion (11), coating delamination (8), water penetration (8), rooflight failure (6), fixings corrosion (4), excessive colour loss (3), fixing failure (2), other substrate corrosion (1), chalking (3), sealant failure (1), condensation (1) and dirt retention (1). A further seven contacts failed to respond to this question.
11. Can you estimate the actual overcoating and ultimate lifetimes?†	10–15 years (1), 16–20 years (6, two as overcoating lifetime), 21–25 years (1), 25–30 years (4, two as overcoating), 30–40 years (3, two as ultimate lifetimes), 40–50 years (1). The remaining contacts offered no figure.
12. Would you use the material again?	Yes (25), yes with reservation (8), no (for PVF$_2$) (1). The remaining two replies did not give this information.

*Each contact was asked for the source of the product(s) used. If the same product or supplier was mentioned in two surveys, it was counted twice in the summary. This summary lists the total number of products used from each country and is intended to give an idea of the proportions supplied from each.

†Respondents were asked to provide figures for both overcoating, and ultimate lifetimes, as for question number (3) above. However, almost all gave only a single figure. Where either overcoating or ultimate lifetimes were specified, this is noted in the summary.

Survey of installers (twenty usable replies)

Question	Summary
1. What products have you used?	
(a) substrate	Galvanised steel (16 replies), aluminium (11), aluminium-coated steel (6), and aluminium–zinc alloy coated steel (6). One reply gave no information.
(b) coating	Plastisol (14), PVF$_2$ (12), Polyester (8), unspecified powder coating (8), abrasion resistant system (8), acrylic (6), organosol (6), silicone–polyester (5), and alkyd (2). One reply gave no information.
(c) process	Coil coated/roll formed (13), powder coated (10), pressed tiles (10) and anodising (1).
2. How long have you been using the products in question?	1–5 years (1), 6–10 years (5), 10–15 years (4), 16–20 years (4) and >20 years (5). The remaining contact gave no figure.
3. What time period do you expect	
(a) until repainting?	10–15 years (3), 10–20 years (1), 10–30 years (1), 16–20 years (3) and 21–25 years (2). Nine replies did not give a figure, and a further felt that the product would not require overcoating.
(b) until sheet replacement?	<20 years (1), 20–30 years (7), 31–40 years (3), 41–50 years (1) and >50 years (1). The remaining seven replies gave no time period.
4. Indicate the supplier of each material*	UK (54 mentions), Sweden (8), Switzerland (2), Belgium (2), France (2), Finland (1) and America (1).
5. For what purpose?	Cladding (15), roofing (17), internal lining (11), in-fill panels (5), curtain walling (5), fascias (1), soffits (1), windows (1) and doors (1). Constructions used: single skin (14 replies), insulation/liner trays (14) and composite panels (13).
6. What types of buildings?	Industrial (17), commercial (17) residential (10), educational (2), leisure (1) and four others. One contact gave no information.
7. In what environments?	Industrial (16), urban (17), rural (14) and coastal (11).
8. Are you aware of any problems encountered with installation?	None (10), edge corrosion and peel (2), damage to sheets (1), handling of long sheets (1), condensation (1), alignment of composite panels (1), excessive gap at composite panels (1), rusting caused by swarf (1) and delivery problems (1).
9. Was any action taken to protect cut edges?	Yes (9), none (5). The remaining six replies made no comment.
10. Have you experienced any problems in service?	Cut edge corrosion (11), coating delamination (11), rooflight failure (8), excessive colour loss (7), fixings corrosion (5), chalking (4), other substrate corrosion (2), water penetration (2), crazing/flaking (2), and fixing failure (2). Three contacts reported no problems and a further two contacts failed to respond to this question.

Continued

Question	Summary
11. Can you estimate the actual overcoating and ultimate lifetimes?†	10–15 years (1), 16–20 years (2) and 21–30 years (3). Eleven contacts stated that they were unable to offer an estimate and the remaining three failed to reply.
12. Would you use the material again?	Yes (16) and yes with reservation (1). The remaining three replies did not give this information.

* Each contact was asked for the source of the product(s) used. If the same product or supplier was mentioned in two surveys, it was counted twice in the summary. This summary lists the total number of products used from each country and is intended to give an idea of the proportions supplied from each.

†Respondents were asked to provide figures for both overcoating, and ultimate lifetimes, as for question number (3) above. However, almost all gave only a single figure. Where either overcoating or ultimate lifetimes were specified, this is noted in the summary.

Survey of occupiers (nine usable replies)

Question	Summary
1. What products have you used?	
(a) substrate	Galvanised steel (6 replies), aluminium (3), aluminium coated steel (1), aluminium/zinc alloy coated steel (1) and steel. One reply gave no information.
(b) coating	Plastisol (6), PVF_2 (4), unspecified powder coating (2) and acrylic (1). One reply gave no information.
(c) process	Coil coated/roll formed (5), powder coated (5) and pressed tiles (3). One reply was unaware of the process used.
2. How long have you been using the products in question?	<1 year (1), 1–5 years (2), 6–10 years (2), 10–15 years (2) and 16–20 years (2).
3. What time period do you expect	
(a) until repainting?	10–15 years (1), 16–20 years (4) 21–25 years (1) and >25 years (1). The remaining two replies did not give a figure.
(b) until sheet replacement?	<20 years (1), 20–30 years (3) and 41–50 years (2). The remaining three replies gave no time period.
4. Indicate the supplier of each material*	UK (12 mentions), Sweden (1) and Belgium (1).
5. For what purpose?	Roofing (8), cladding (7), internal lining (3), curtain walling (2) and in-fill panels (1). Constructions used: Composite panels (3), insulation/liner tray (2) and single skin (2). Five replies failed to describe the method of construction.
6. What types of buildings?	Industrial (4), commercial (5) residential (4) and bus station (1).
7. In what environments?	Urban (4), coastal (3), rural (3) and industrial (2). One contact failed to give this information.
8. Are you aware of any problems encountered with installation?	None (4), rusting caused by swarf (1), tile damage from fixing nails (1), coating failure in heat (1) and condensation causing coating failure. Three contacts gave no information.
9. Was any action taken to protect cut edges?	None (3), yes (2). The remaining four replies made no comment.
10. Have you experienced any problems in service?	None (3), excessive fading (3), fixings corrosion (2), water penetration (2), cut edge corrosion (2), coating delamination (1), chalking (1), rooflight failure (1), other substrate corrosion (1), crazing/flaking (1), fixing failure (1), organic growth (1) and difficulty in cleaning (1).
11. Can you estimate the actual overcoating and ultimate lifetimes?[2]	25 years + (1), 21–25 years for overcoating (1 reply) and 41–50 years ultimate life (1). The remaining seven contacts offered no opinions.
12. Would you use the material again?	Yes (7) and yes with reservation (1). The remaining replies did not give this information.

*Each contact was asked for the source of the product(s) used. If the same product or supplier was mentioned in two surveys, it was counted twice in the summary. This summary list the total number of products used from each country and is intended to give an idea of the proportions supplied from each.

†Respondents were asked to provide figures for both overcoating, and ultimate lifetimes, as for question number (3) above. However, almost all gave only a single figure. Where either overcoating or ultimate lifetimes were specified, this is noted in the summary.

International survey (ten replies)

Question	1	2
1. Country of origin.	Ireland.	Australia.
2. What coil coatings are used in your country?	Acrylic and plastisol.	Most commonly silicone – polyester, but also polyester and acrylic.
3. On what substrates?	Aluminium, galvanised steel and aluminium – zinc alloy coated steel.	Aluminium – zinc alloy (50–60% Al) coated steel.
4. What processes are used on the coated materials?	Roll forming, pressing, composite panels and secret fix systems.	Roll forming, pressing and composite panels.
5. What types of powder coatings are used?	No experience.	Polyester and thermoplastic products on aluminium and galvanised steel.
6. Are other relevant coatings used?	No.	No.
7. Describe in detail the most widely used product in your country.	1.5 mm galvanised steel coated on the face side with plastisol and on the reverse side with an acrylic. The product is imported for use as roofing and cladding in commercial, industrial and leisure buildings.	Locally produced 0.5–0.9 mm aluminium – zinc alloy coated steel for use as roofing and cladding. Primary use is light industrial, but also examples of heavy industrial, leisure, commercial, educational and housing.
8. For how long has this product been used?	5 years.	20 years.
9. What life do you expect from this material?	15 years.	Depends on exposure, particularly in coastal regions. Normally >25 years, but reduced to ten in exposed marine locations.
10. Is this achieved?	Not known.	See above.
11. What failures of the product have been experienced?	None.	Poor performance in coastal areas, with corrosion on unwashed surfaces, especially where a tight radius on corners has been used.
12. Is there a paint system available for routine maintenance on-site?	Yes — plastisol based (interpreted as a coating **for** plastisol).	Original coating gives better performance, but still gives trouble on tight radius on roll forming.

Continued

Question	3	4
1. Country of origin.	Austria.	Norway.
2. What coil coatings are used in your country?	Polyester, silicone – polyester and PVF$_2$ – acrylic.	Organosol, acrylic, polyester, silicone – polyester, plastisol, abrasion-resistant system and PVF$_2$ – acrylic (50:50).
3. On what substrates?	Aluminium.	Aluminium, galvanised steel and aluminium – zinc alloy coated steel (55% Al, 43.4% Zn, 1.6% Si).
4. What processes are used on the coated materials?	Roll forming, pressing and composite panels.	Roll forming.
5. What types of powder coatings are used?	Polyester on aluminium and galvanised steel.	Polyester on aluminium.
6. Are other relevant coatings used?	No.	No.
7. Describe in detail the most widely used product in your country.	Locally produced with a 20 μm coating on the face side and 5 μm on the reverse side. Used as both roofing and cladding in commercial, educational leisure and industrial buildings.	Imported 0.4–1.0 mm steel coated on the face side with 200 μm plastisol and on the reverse side with a 10–20 μm coating. Used primarily for cladding and roofing of leisure and industrial buildings but also in commercial, educational and housing projects.
8. For how long has this product been used?	25 years.	Since the 1980s.
9. What life do you expect from this material?	Circa 100 years.	30 years.
10. Is this achieved?	Yes.	No.
11. What failures of the product have been experienced?	None.	Corrosion at edges and discolouring of plastisol.
12. Is there a paint system available for routine maintenance on-site?	No information given.	Not known.

Continued

Question	5	6
1. Country of origin.	Austria.	Austria.
2. What coil coatings are used in your country?	Not known.	Not known.
3. On what substrates?	Not known.	Not known.
4. What processes are used on the coated materials?	Not known.	Composite panels and secret fix systems. The products are fabricated from steel prior to coating — no bending or drilling is carried out after coating.
5. What types of powder coatings are used?	Polyester on aluminium.	Not known.
6. Are other relevant coatings used?	No.	Vitreous enamel coating on steel and/or stainless steel.
7. Describe in detail the most widely used product in your country	Locally produced 80 µm polyester powder coating on 2–4 mm aluminium. Used as cladding for commercial, leisure industrial, housing and educational projects.	Locally produced 1.5–2 mm steel sheet, coated on the face side with a two-coat (150 µm ground enamel + 150–200 µm vitreous enamel) system and on the reverse with a 150 µm coating. The product is used mainly as cladding but also as roofing, for commercial, educational, leisure, industrial, high rise residential and housing projects, including marine locations.
8. For how long has this product been used?	20 years.	Approx 50 years.
9. What life do you expect from this material?	Approx 40 years.	At least 30 years.
10. Is this achieved?	Not yet known, but assume so.	Yes.
11. What failures of the product have been experienced?	No failures, although some chalking has been found to occur.	Slight corrosion of underlying steel at chipped areas.
12. Is there a paint system available for routine maintenance on-site?	No.	No — not necessary.

Continued

Question	7	8
1. Country of origin.	Austria.	South Africa.
2. What coil coatings are used in your country?	Not known.	Plastisol, polyester and silicone – polyester (95%).
3. On what substrates?	Not known.	Aluminium and galvanised steel.
4. What processes are used on the coated materials?	Not known.	Roll forming, pressing into tiles, composite panels and secret fix systems.
5. What types of powder coatings are used?	Polyester on aluminium.	No experience.
6. Are other relevant coatings used?	No.	No.
7. Describe in detail the most widely used product in your country.	Locally produced 80 µm polyester powder coating on 3 mm aluminium. Used as cladding on leisure, commercial, educational, and industrial buildings.	Locally produced 20 µm silicone – polyester coil coating on Z275 galvanised steel. Used as both roofing and cladding, primarily for leisure and industrial buildings, but also for commercial, industrial domestic and marine installations.
8. For how long has this product been used?	About 20 years.	Galvanised steel about 40 years. Pre-painted about 25 years.
9. What life do you expect from this material?	About 20 years.	About 30 years, with maintenance.
10. Is this achieved?	Yes.	At least this period, when maintained.
11. What failures of the product have been experienced?	None.	Mostly corrosion failures — bad detailing at end laps, chalking, flaking of plastisol, cut edges and failures at coastal locations — need better product.
12. Is there a paint system available for routine maintenance on site?	No information given.	Yes — handled by paint suppliers.

Continued

Question	9	10
1. Country of origin.	New Zealand.	Germany.
2. What coil coatings are used in your country?	Acrylic, polyester, plastisol, silicone–polyester, PVF_2, organosol and laminates.	Acrylic, polyester, organosol, silicone–polyester, plastisol and PVF_2.
3. On what substrates?	Aluminium, galvanised steel, Zincalume and Galvalume.	Aluminium, galvanised steel and aluminium–zinc alloy coated steel.
4. What processes are used on the coated materials?	Roll forming, pressing, composites and secret fix. Also gutters and drainpipes.	Roll forming, composite panels and secret-fix systems.
5. What types of powder coatings are used?	Polyester, thermoplastic and epoxy/polyester hybrids on aluminium and galvanised steel.	No experience.
6. Are other relevant coatings used?	No.	No.
7. Describe in detail the most widely used product in your country.	Locally produced acrylic or silicone–polyester, 40 μm overall, on 0.4–0.55 mm galvanised steel. Reverse side is typically 30 μm but can be as face. Used as cladding and roofing mainly on commercial and housing, but also all other low rise type buildings.	Locally produced product (no details given) used as cladding and roofing for mainly light and heavy industrial, but also leisure buildings.
8. For how long has this product been used?	20 years for coil coating. Sheet galvanised steel has been the dominant roofing material in NZ for >100 years.	30–35 years.
9. What life do you expect from this material?	Varies with installation, maintenance and location. Unmaintained marine — 15 years. Well maintained inland — 50–100 years. Maintenance includes repainting where necessary.	No information given.
10. Is this achieved?	In general yes, when specified and maintained properly.	No information given.
11. What failures of the product have been experienced?	Varies, but usually depends on use, rather than product. Chalking is common, and is largely expected. Staining during roll forming has been encountered. Most common corrosion is where coating is microcracked due to forming to too tight a radius. Also base metal corrosion where material is sheltered and not washed in service.	No information given.
12. Is there a paint system available for routine maintenance on-site?	Yes — a two-coat acrylic.	No information given.

Miscellaneous surveys (eleven replies)

Question	1	2
1. With what products are you familiar?		
a) substrate	Aluminium	Aluminium
b) coating	Polyester & PVF$_2$	Polyester (80–100 μm), abrasion-resistant system (20 μm) and PVF$_2$ (25–35 μm).
c) process	Coil coated/roll formed.	Coil coated/roll formed, powder coated and wet spray.
2. How long, and in what context, have you been using the products in question?	Ten years, as a distributor and stockholder.	13 years, as a panel producer.
3. What period do you expect		
a) until repainting?	20 years	No figure given
b) until sheet replacement?	30 years.	30 years.
4. Indicate the supplier of each material.	France (1).	UK (more than 3), France (2) and Germany (1).
5. What colours have you used?	Various.	Seven colours listed.
6. For what purpose?	Cladding, roofing, curtain walling, in-fill panels and internal lining, as composite panels.	Cladding, curtain walling and in-fill panels, as composite panels.
7. What types of buildings?	Commercial and industrial.	Commercial.
8. In what environments?	Rural, urban and industrial.	Coastal and tropical.
9. Are you aware of any problems encountered with installation?	No.	No information given.
10. Was any action taken to protect cut edges?	No.	Silicone seal — no problems reported.
11. Have you experienced any problems in service?	No information given.	Minor coating delamination after 5–6 years in a tropical coastal climate — paint blistering in panel folds.
12. Can you estimate the actual overcoating and ultimate lifetimes?	No.	No.
13. Would you use the material again?	Yes.	Yes.
14. Any other comments?	No.	No.

Continued

Question	3
1. What products have you used?	
a) substrate	Aluminium.
b) coating	Polyester.
c) process	Powder coated.
2. How long, and in what context, have you been using the products in question?	4 years, as an aluminium systems company.
3. What time period do you expect	
a) until repainting?	25 years.
b) until sheet replacement?	Not stated.
4. Indicate the supplier of each material.	UK (2).
5. What colours have you used?	Various.
6. For what purpose?	Curtain walling.
7. What types of buildings?	Commercial and industrial.
8. In what environments?	Rural, urban, industrial and coastal.
9. Are you aware of any problems encountered with installation?	No.
10. Was any action taken to protect cut edges?	No.
11. Have you experienced any problems in service?	No information given.
12. Can you estimate the actual overcoating and ultimate lifetimes?	No.
13. Would you use the material again?	Yes.
14. Any other comments?	No.

A further five companies replied, but had no relevant information to offer. In addition, technical literature was supplied from three manufacturers of ancillary materials (sealants etc.) used in this product area.

APPENDIX 3: Reproduction of Annex E from pr EN 505 and pr 508-1: 1996 (Roofing products from metal sheet—steel)

**Annex E
(informative):
Durability of organic
coatings**

Note. This annex will be obsolete when EN 10169 Parts 1 and 2 are published.

This annex provides guidance on the durability of organic coatings but for more detailed information on a particular coating it is essential to contact the profiler or the coated steel manufacturer. Specific geographical and climatic conditions should be considered.

Modern coatings can provide functional protection for up to 30 years without major repainting apart from that given to exposed cut edges. However during that time it is probable that some change will have taken place in the appearance. This could include loss of gloss, chalking, fading or slight change of colour. None of these will reduce the functional aspect of the coating. Table E.1 gives guidance on the expected life without serious deterioration for the frequently used coatings.

The durability data quoted in Table E.1 refers to the organic coated external surface of the roof sheet.

Edge corrosion is inhibited by the sacrificial action or barrier protection of the metallic coating on the steel. The onset of edge corrosion can be delayed by the application of additional edge protection or by bending the edge down to improve drainage.

The periods quoted are maxima for the whole of Europe; manufacturers should be consulted for the period appropriate to a specific country, its local weather conditions and any national regulations which control

Table E.1: Guide to probable durability of coatings

Environment	Northern Europe (generally North of 45° latitude North*)			Southern Europe (generally South of 45° latitude North*)		
	Rural	Urban/ industrial	Marine/coastal	Rural	Urban/ industrial	Marine/coastal
Polyester and silicone polyester	20	20	10	10	10	5
PVDF	20	20	10	15	15	5
PVF(F)	25	25	20	25	25	20
PVC(P)	30	30	20	20	20	15
Multicoat systems	30	25	15	25	25	15
Multi layer	30	25	25	25	25	20

*The demarcation between the two zones is not precise and judgement should be used in deciding which to adopt. In any case of doubt the figures for Southern Europe should be used.

either the minimum design life or definition of permitted changes in coating appearance.

Table E.1 is presented as a guide to help in primary selection of the coating and to give an indication of the probable durability.

The performance of coatings especially PVC(P) and polyester vary depending on their pigmentation. While in general light tones perform better than dark tones there might be exceptions. Black PVC(P) for instance is a good performer because its pigmentation acts as an effective UV-barrier.

Paint systems not included in the table should be rated accordingly to suppliers' guidelines.